Written Communication for DATA PROCESSING

Rändi Sigmund Smith

VAN NOSTRAND REINHOLD COMPANY

NEW YORK   CINCINNATI   ATLANTA   DALLAS   SAN FRANCISCO
LONDON   TORONTO   MELBOURNE

Van Nostrand Reinhold Company Regional Offices:
New York   Cincinnati   Atlanta   Dallas   San Francisco

Van Nostrand Reinhold Company International Offices:
London   Toronto   Melbourne

Library of Congress Catalog Card Number: 76-44292
ISBN: 0-442-27793-8

Manufactured in the United States of America

Published by Van Nostrand Reinhold Company
450 West 33rd Street, New York, N.Y. 10001

Published simultaneously in Canada by Van Nostrand Reinhold Ltd.

15 14 13 12 11 10 9 8 7 6 5 4 3 2 1

Library of Congress Cataloging in Publication Data

Smith, Randi S
    Written communication for data processing.

    Includes index.
    1.   Commercial correspondence.   2.   Business re-
port writing.   3.   Communication in management.
4.   Electronic data processing departments.   I.   Title.
HF5718.S6   651.7′5   76-44292
ISBN 0-442-27793-8

Contents

v

REPORT WRITING / 161

1
Why Them?

Corporations and other large organizations have taken written communication for granted since the Industrial Revolution. Why now is there such concern on the part of contemporary management with the *effectiveness* of what's being written?

Consider this. Over 30 billion pieces of written material are distributed in the United States each year and the number is growing. Some of this, of course, represents checks, financial statements—not something someone had to sit down, think through, and write at one end of a communication channel or something someone must sit down, read, and act upon at the other end of the communication channel. The bulk of it, however, and estimates run as high as 80%, does represent business letters, memorandums, and reports—documents someone had to think through and write, documents someone had to read and act upon. The word count alone in the business communications distributed is estimated at 10,000 times the number of words in all the fiction published in the United States each year. It's a staggering number of words, and you are probably in a better position than I am to say how many are worthwhile.

Most of us in data processing environments write more memorandums (interoffice communication vehicles, IOCs) than the traditional business letter. Many organizations are attempting actually to count these documents, and large corporations now find they can easily distribute one million or more memorandums in just one year. *One million or more*, and not necessarily single-page memorandums. Writing has become the biggest business in big business, and, again, you are in a better position than I to evaluate what is written. How many of the memos crossing your desk are necessary? How many serve only to fill the circular file?

If we agree writing is big business, we must recognize that big business means big expense. Nationwide surveys, conducted to pin down just how much writing is costing us, have turned up some surprising figures.

Currently, a half-page, 175-word letter or memorandum can range in cost from $1 to an almost unbelievable high of $9.60. In most data processing areas, our cost is running much closer to the $9.60 figure than to the $1 figure, if for no other reason than much of what we write is longer than one-half page, 175 words. Think about it. What can you do with one-half page, 175 words except, perhaps, announce a departmental picnic?

The nationwide average cost is $2.50. This means that each time you sit down to write, your organization is tapped for at least $2.50 in administrative cost. Now we're not talking about the added expenses of typing, paper, and distribution. The $2.50 is your price tag—your valuable time, the desk you sit at, the light you see by.

It doesn't sound like much, does it? Two bucks, plus 50 pennies. But have you thought about how much you write? How many memos or letters do you write on a daily basis? One? Ten? Even in data processing, where we may write nothing for awhile and then do a great deal of writing, the numbers are averaging out to between two to four documents a day per employee.

Let's carry things to an extreme, just to make a point. Suppose you write a simple, informational memorandum, one-half page, 175 words. Your cost in orginating the memo is $2.50. If you wrote 25 of these a day, 300 working days a year, it could cost your organization $18,750.00 a year to keep you writing. Not to do any other part of your job—just to shuffle paper. Frightening isn't it? This money has to come from somewhere. We all know it isn't going into salaries. Also, at these prices, any corporation is certainly going to be concerned with getting its money's worth.

There's more. Up to now, we've only been considering one end of a communication channel. Communication, by definition, is *interaction between people*. This means, if we're going to take time to write, hopefully someone at the other end of the communication channel will read, understand, and act upon what we've written. The reader's commitment is as expensive and time-consuming as the writer's. It is an equal administrative bombshell.

Suppose we again write our simple, informational memorandum, one-half page, 175 words. We send this memo to 50 people on a distribution list. Allowing only 15 minutes per recipient to read and act upon our memorandum, we've accounted for 12½ person hours of time. People spent these hours just reading what we've written. What is the administrative cost to your organization of 12½ used-up hours?

Now, I'm not suggesting it will take anyone 15 minutes to read the average memorandum. The key words in our formula are *act upon*. If you write someone, you usually expect something to happen, don't you? You are looking for a decision or you hope to elicit information vital to your job. At the very least, you hope to increase your reader's level of comprehension about a given subject. With what you set out to accomplish in most cases, 15 minutes is not that long.

We've already discussed how much time we spend writing. How much time do you spend reading? Seems like all your time, doesn't it? In technical areas, we can spend 40 to 60% of our time clearing out an in-box or reading existing material. It may be that our greatest investment of time and administrative cost sits at this end of the communication channel.

This leads me to a maxim that is not popular, but has proven in my personal experience to be true. *People tend to get the type of communication they deserve.* What does this say about what you're currently reading? If you're like most people, probably not much. Think about it, however. If what we write makes sense and is easy to understand and use, we have left our reader no option but to respond effectively to us. In fact, in many instances we could make it unnecessary for our reader to respond at all. That has to sound good to those of you buried in a paper avalanche.

Again, let's take an example of what poor or unnecessary written communication costs on the reader side. Suppose 25 ineffective memorandums are received by 50 individuals in your organization in one month. I'm sure each of us receives at least 25 in any month. Because these memos are ineffective, your company is out *40 wasted person days.* That time is gone. So is the money it represents. What about the additional damage in frustration and low morale among employees? Data processing environments run on deadlines. You may never miss one, but they are missed occasionally, and many by less than 40 days. Perhaps the biggest bottleneck to productivity in data processing is not lack of technical competency or creativity, but what we write or don't write and what we read.

Come back a minute to the word *ineffective*. I don't want to get hung up on semantics, and each of us might define ineffective somewhat differently. When I say *ineffective* relative to any communication vehicle—letter, memorandum, or report—I mean the letter, memo, or report did *not* accomplish its original objective the first time around.

Now we all know how this happens. I write a memo and send it to my user, Hank Jones. I don't do as good a job as I might. I leave out some stage-setting information. My request is confusing. Naturally, Hank does not understand my memo. He can't do as I require because he's not sure of my needs or position. At the very least, what will Hank do? He may call me for clarification. Probably, however, Hank will write me a memorandum in response. He has nothing else to do with his day, and it is standard operating procedure anyway. I see three, four, five memos going between the same two people on the same subject, and neither of them understands things any better after the fifth than after the first. Obviously, this is a waste of my time and Hank's. But the problem to us and to our organization goes much deeper than that.

After the fifth memo, when I know Hank still doesn't get it, what do I think of Hank as a person? He's capable, professional, and organized, right? Wrong. I know he's a turkey. The reverse, unfortunately, is also true. Hank is convinced I'm a total idiot and difficult to get along with under any circumstances.

The working relationship between two individuals has been destroyed—a crucial link snapped in the organization's structure.

It gets worse. What do I now think of the competency of Hank's entire department or area? I probably believe they're brainless and impossible. What does Hank think of my data processing group? Does he conclude we're good at our jobs, able to provide the service he needs and expects? He does not. Hank and I will both approach any future communication with each other or anyone else from our respective areas expecting trouble. Because we expect it, that's exactly what we'll get. We have not only annihilated the cooperative connection between two people, we have sabotaged the necessary rapport between two parts of the corporate anatomy, crippling the whole.

No company can afford such a penalty for poorly written communication, and most organizations have come, at last, to know it.

2
Why Us?

Poor communication is the single greatest cause of data processing catastrophes—in systems development, operations, system modification, system maintenance, and DP management. The costs of poor communication in any technical environment are incalculable. Yet we in the data processing community continue to accept poorly organized, badly written, and incomplete documents, perhaps believing nothing can be done about the situation.

I think we've been brainwashed. It's that simple. Consider the "everyone knows technical people can't write" axiom. Trapped by such a self-fulfilling prophecy (and handy cop-out), data processors are traditionally reluctant even to try to express themselves in prose. Certainly, we take letter, memorandum, and report writing for granted. It's the grunt part of an otherwise creative job, viewed much more as a chore than as an opportunity.

Perhaps we should take a closer look at why we write. Do we have any personal stake in what we put on paper? Is our written language the key to higher productivity and fewer crisis-laden workdays?

Certainly, in any organization, what we write reaches more people than what we say. Often it touches individuals—customers, support personnel, management decision-makers—we may never have the opportunity to deal with verbally.

Within our own data processing environments, what we write has a tendency to hang around forever. It even can become a training vehicle for new people—often their only guide to satisfactory understanding of job responsibility. How well did these "training vehicles" work for you when you were new to your job? Have you ever tried to work with someone else's System Documentation? Much of what I see indicates we are simply passing on bad habits and complicating an already difficult orientation process.

What about our writing as a personal reflection of self? In most organizations, our own abilities and talents are evaluated more often by what we write than by any other criteria. People make judgments about who we are and what we are capable of accomplishing based on what they see on paper.

Remember the old saying that no idea is ever brilliant unless we can get it across to someone else in a way he or she can easily understand, accept, and utilize it? This adage is truer in data processing environments than in any other. No matter how creative or experienced we are technically, if others cannot understand, accept, and implement what we provide, we are being brilliant in a closet. How many sound, innovative data processing ideas are rejected, not because of lack of feasibility, but because of slipshod, unenthusiastic communication?

Here's an example. We complain about psychological barriers between ourselves and our users or customers. Yet our writing, or the lack of it, is building the very walls that frustrate us. Isn't it true that the individuals who must utilize a data processing service are usually people with a minimal amount of background or experience in data processing? They don't understand what data processing can or cannot do and we rarely enlighten them. We all know, however, what inevitably happens in the end. Not understanding, they resist, misuse, or underutilize the service we struggle to provide. The system fails, no matter how well it was designed.

Data processors need to learn to define goals clearly and specify results on paper, bringing customers and support groups directly into the mainstream of data processing experience. This does require mastering communication skills. More than anything, it requires a commitment to improved communication on the part of each one of us, and I believe we can do it.

Technical people can learn to write. Many of us simply have never been afforded the opportunity to learn. As a start, I have listed (in Chapters 3 through 8) the criteria used by consultants like myself to evaluate the writing in letters, memorandums, and reports. These criteria are an excellent check on your personal writing skill. A review of them should help you develop a mental red pencil, enabling you to organize your thoughts, vocabulary, and sentences without much hassle. There will be no more ''insert A, delete B, cross out page 3,'' just straightforward, practical writing designed to meet your objectives.

Once you have the writing fundamentals in mind, we can proceed to identify (in Chapters 9 through 17) the major points in the data processing life cycle and define the problems inherent in each. Simple guidelines are presented for meeting each problem and producing clear and concise documents that will be read and understood. Each example is based on actual cases, starting with a hypothetical user request for service and following it through each stage of service development and presentation.

Chapters 18 through 22 deal with an assignment we all dislike—the writing of reports. Techniques presented apply to any management report from Feasibility Studies and Proposals to Forecasting Objectives. Planning hints, organizational structure, actual writing procedures, and some ways to cheat are there for you to try.

There is one thing my years of teaching experience have taught me—something I would like to share with you as you begin. The ability to communicate effectively on paper is a skill like any other. It can be easily learned and, then, with practice, become almost instinctive, like riding a bike or playing the piano. There is nothing esoteric about good written communication. It is not magic. It is, simply, a crucial technical and administrative tool—one we have done without in data processing for far too long.

SIX KEYS TO SUCCESS

Chapters 3-8 contain the criteria used to evaluate business and technical writing. Each tip or technique is presented in one of six specific Keys to show how it should be used and why each is considered important.

3
Key I—Making Valid Assumptions About The Reader

In evaluating someone's written material, I look first to see if this approach has been utilized. Good writers make valid assumptions about their readers in order to determine what needs to be said and how the content should be presented. The decision-making involved is a mental discipline and must be completed prior to the actual writing of any document.

A. Always know who and what.

This is a basic tenet in any form of communication—written or spoken—and it sounds patently obvious. We have to know who we are writing to before we can address our document, and we must know what we're going to say in order to write it. I wonder, however, if this awareness is as patently obvious as it appears.

For one thing, data processors are in love with initials. Take mine—R. S. Smith. Who is R. S. Smith? Do you know? My guess is you'll come up with Robert or Richard before Rändi. Suppose you need to call me. Who do you ask for? R. S. Smith? In any department in any large organization, there are probably four of us. Which do you want? Most companies use first names, no matter what the rank. Not knowing mine puts you at an immediate disadvantage. You don't know if I'm male or female, and, if female, whether I'm Ms., Miss, or Mrs. This creates difficulty even in using my last name properly. When someone writes you from outside your organization and only provides his or her initials, some problem does exist in determining name. I consistently find, however, people writing on a regular basis to individuals within their own organizations whom they can only distinguish by initials. These writers don't know who their readers are and haven't taken the simple steps of reaching for a telephone directory or asking someone in order to find out. (Of course, some companies compound the problem by using initials in their telephone directories.)

What is the first thing we find out about anyone we meet in a verbal context? Isn't it that person's name? Channels of communication begin with establishing of identity. For example, have you ever been to a meeting where there are four other participants—you don't know three of them and no one introduces you? Are you an active participant? I doubt it. In that situation, we hold back, waiting to see who these people are and where they're coming from. We don't communicate well without names, even in a give-and-take verbal situation. Imagine how much greater the barrier when we remain anonymous on paper. Remember, communication is defined as "interaction between people." Without names, there are no people and no communication. There is only a faceless nonentity in one bureaucracy shuffling paper to a faceless nonentity in another.

What else about a person would be a clue to what he or she needs and expects? Certainly, it helps to know an individual's title or position. No title gives you a biography, but it should indicate responsibility and interests—important clues as to how your letter, memorandum, or report will be used.

I also like to know the department my reader represents, although this information is often omitted, especially from distribution lists. If a reader is from an area outside data processing, we then know to watch our jargon and limit our technical shorthand.

Reaching the right "who" is equally important. Have you ever put time and effort into a document asking for a decision—one you needed badly—only to find out the individual you addressed was not the one to make such a decision? Perhaps you also devised an excellent memo guaranteed to elicit crucial information from a user, only to find your reader was not the person in the know? Well, then you should easily see that the time to research the "who" is prior to writing. We don't always know "who," and until we recognize that fact and take it seriously enough to correct it, our writing will continue to frustrate both us and our reader.

Once we establish "who," we are in a better position to determine "what." Unless you can define your specific objective—what you wish to accomplish— prior to writing, you either are not ready to write or you may not need to write at all. Certainly, what we don't know ourselves, we can never make clear to our reader.

Have you ever received a letter or memorandum, read it, and then thought to yourself, "Eh!"—"So what?" Most people have. Isn't it true, in that instance, that the writer could not have defined his or her objective in writing in the first place? If the writer had, you would know "so what?"—probably "why me?"—or you would not have received the letter or memo in the first place.

Perhaps the best example of failure to define objective honestly is the famous, or infamous, Memorandum to File. I hope you've never heard of it. If you work for a large organization, however, I'm sure you have.

The Memorandum to File is written to document anything that takes place in a verbal context—meetings, telephone conversations, trips to the men's room. I see thousands each year, and I know why the Memo to File is written. We write it because we've all been burned at least once by taking verbal acceptance for granted. Emblazoned in neon lights in every data processing area I visit is the motto "CYA" or "Protect thyself" (if you'll accept that translation). That is our objective in writing the Memorandum to File, and by defining it, we can limit the number we write. The Memo to File need only be written if one or both of two things occur in a verbal context:

1. *A decision is reached.* Decisions must be documented. We know how easily unrecorded ones are forgotten or distorted.

2. *Responsibility is assigned or assumed.* Here written confirmation is crucial. Nothing is more easily misunderstood or denied than specific responsibility, particularly should problems develop.

If one or both of these two elements do not occur, however, why are we writing the Memo to File? Isn't it force of habit, and a waste of our time and our reader's? Decisions and responsibility are where we get sandbagged. With any other area of conversation, I can see making notes in a working file for your own use. I cannot see the writing and distribution of a formal memorandum.

Try defining objective carefully. Ask yourself, "Why am I taking my valuable time to write?" and if you don't have a good answer, don't.

B. Visualize your reader.

Knowing who and what, we should take a moment to visualize our reader. Of course, we are not considering physical characteristics—he's 5'10" and bald—but we are concerned with his or her working environment. What is your reader dealing with day to day? What is the situation in which he or she is currently operating? What are your reader's responsibilities?

This is valuable insight. We tend to formulate our solutions or suggestions at our desks under familiar working conditions. We need to visualize our reader's surroundings in order mentally to drop anything we offer into the environment where it is actually going to be utilized.

C. Think as your reader will think.

This is the most important rule in effective written communication, and there are no exceptions. It is *always* the writer's responsibility to step into the reader's frame of reference. It is *never* the reader's responsibility to step into the writer's frame of reference. In data processing, particularly, that makes good sense.

If our readers had our technical expertise, our level of experience, who would they not need? If they could get what they required on their own, they certainly would not come to us. We'd be out of a job. The only way we can successfully present any data processing service is to hit our reader where he or she lives—and the responsibility for finding common ground is ours.

D. Think in terms of specifics.

In thinking as our reader will think, we must stay with specific information. Generalities are a great danger to effective written communication. We use them, I suspect, because they're easy. Any one of us could come up with a couple of sensational generalities, particularly if our fog index is high. Unfortunately, generalities are not convincing. Sooner or later, we must go in with specifics, often to someone who has already made at least a mental decision based on the incomplete information provided.

Let's take an example. Say I am a user, and I come to you with a problem. If I could solve it myself, you know I'd be off kingdom-building on my own. I certainly wouldn't come to you. Obviously, then, I need your professional assistance. You know your job. You can do your homework and come back to me saying: "Rändi, you should move in the direction of point Y. If you and your people get to point Y, the problem is solved." Now you're absolutely correct. I should be at point Y. But are you expecting me to figure out how to get there? If I knew, I wouldn't have to come to you in the first place. You've made my job in implementing your solution so difficult, I'm going to reject your excellent suggestion with all the customary excuses—"You didn't understand my problem"— "My people (or management) can't live with that."

You're an experienced data processor. Why not offer me specifics in the beginning? You could tell me, "Rändi, you should move from point A to point B to point C—this will put you at point Y—and this is what you can expect when you get there." Now it's a whole different ball game. You have made my job as easy as possible, and I should at least try your solution prior to complaining about it—great progress for some users.

You even have another option using specifics. Suppose you have dealt with me before and you know I'm tough to get along with. There are some people like that in any organization. Go one step further. Say to me, "Rändi, you should move from point A to point B to point C—this will put you at point Y—and this is what you can expect when you get to point Y—*and* this is what will happen if you do not go to point Y." Now, for the first time, you have me or any user making administrative decisions, fully cognizant of the consequences of not accepting your professional recommendation. How many times do users (or any readers) make bad decisions simply because they do not understand the ramifications of not taking a certain action? Yet who is the only one who could have told me what would happen if I did not reach point Y? It's you, and when I don't accept your solution and my original problem becomes a full-blown crisis, I'll be back saying, "Why didn't you tell me?" Sounds only too familiar, doesn't it?

I know it takes more time to come up with specific detail. It takes additional effort. I have never understood, however, why we never have time in data processing to come up with specifics at the initiation of a project or service, but we always have time to patch, rationalize, and redesign. To me, the trade-off is greatly in favor of investing the time in the beginning when the communication channel and our reader's mind are both still open.

E. Anticipate the reader's questions and objections.

We should be knowledgeable enough to anticipate our reader's questions and objections and answer them in our original document. In written communication—without the give and take of face-to-face discussion—your first shot is your best shot. Consider your reader's mental attitude, then write persuasively by providing full information and confronting negative issues head-on.

Take complaints. Say I come to you with a complaint and you respond without considering my viewpoint or the underlying source of my objections. Do I accept your explanation—rational and correct though it may be? Probably not. In most organizations, I rewrite my complaint, and, since I didn't get what I was looking for from you, I bounce it up one administrative level. Your boss now responds, probably again without considering my (or my boss's) questions and level of dissatisfaction. How will my entire area ultimately view your department's "rational" explanation? Does it remain an honest explanation pointing the way to a mutually acceptable solution, or has it just become *another* excuse?

We spend a great deal of time in data processing rationalizing errors. The best way to handle a legitimate complaint is the honest written response: "You're right. I'm sorry it happened. This is the action I'm taking to correct it and this is what I am doing to see it does not occur again." If you take this approach, what have you left your reader to say? "Thank you" is about the only response. Instead of lessened credibility, you create increased respect.

F. What are your reader's assumptions about you?

If we are making assumptions about our reader, it's a good bet he or she is making assumptions about us. Where the reader's assumptions are valid and his or her expectations realistic, I'm sure we all try to meet them. This is not where the bodies are buried. Our problems start when the reader's expectations are unrealistic and their assumptions distorted. Now nothing we offer will satisfy.

Unfortunately, in data processing, we often do this to ourselves. I follow many memorandums and other communication vehicles from data processing areas into user departments and the tone alone frequently suggests: "Here I am, great problem solver of the western world. I'm going to take your problem, handle it better than it's ever been handled and aren't you lucky I'm here.'' Trying to live up to that image has certainly hurt our batting average.

Consider these opening sentences . . .

"This is to inform you . . ." Doesn't that sound somewhat arbitrary? I think it suggests a message in the beak of a dove.

"You will . . . " This one is not even addressed to me, and my immediate reaction was, "You want to bet?" Imagine user reactions.

We are adept in data processing at spelling out what we will do and what our users must do. But to ensure realistic expectations on the part of those we deal with, we must also be willing to detail what is not possible, what we will not do, and what the user cannot do. Far too many users find out what is *not* going to happen after the fact. We did not say it wasn't, so their assumption inevitably is that it is. We are the only ones who can explain limitations—technical and otherwise—and we should do so in the beginning, making sure all of our reader's expectations are at least within the realm of the possible.

G. Don't forget readers plural.

In many instances, we find ourselves dealing not with one reader, but a group of readers—perhaps on a distribution list or in a committee situation. Can we make valid assumptions when we have more than one reader? The answer is yes. Even though our multiple readers may have varying frames of reference or even different levels of comprehension, we can still reach them all and do it with one document.

The solution is to remember the most important criterion used in judging anything written in a business context. *Does it work?* No one in business is concerned with deathless prose or cries of "author, author" from the entire room. (If this is your concern as a writer, write short stories or the great American novel in your spare time.) What business readers demand is usability, and what works for your reader is right.

Let's take an example. Say you hold a meeting attended by three departments in your organization—the user, an operations group, and a development area. All three will be involved in some aspect of the project or service under consideration, and in the course of your discussion, decisions are reached, responsibility is assigned or assumed. You know you must document, yet each of your readers represents a different frame of reference, a different level of technical understanding. How do you reach each of them, in a way best suited to their needs and comprehension, and still write only one memorandum?

You certainly do not want to prepare a "minutes of the meeting." Any of you who receive these know how hard they are to use. You skim through, looking for information pertinent to you and your people, missing most of the rest. Why not structure your document with headings, the name of each department, perhaps—user, operations, development? Under each heading, you can arrange material necessary to that reader, using terminology and materials you know he or she will understand.

At the least, you will get a more thorough reading. Suppose I'm in the operations area. Even if my group appears last in your memo, I will go to my section first and scrutinize all decisions and responsibility directly related to my concerns. Once my mental questions about my commitment are answered, I am more likely to go to the beginning of your document and thoughtfully consider the user and development involvement. Your readers in the other area will do exactly the same. You have reached three readers, three frames of reference and comprehension levels, with one document, and the communication succeeds, because your memo is easily utilized—it works.

Readers with diversified needs and dissimilar comprehension levels can be found even within our own data processing departments. Suppose I need to disseminate information through varying levels within my department, from the people on the firing line up to the individual at the highest level. All my readers are data processors—they work together—yet their levels of understanding and the ways in which they must utilize what I provide are going to differ.

Take the people on the firing line. They will require detail, and probably lots of it, as they are actually going to be doing the work involved.

What about the person at the top, however? We all know in technical areas that the further removed one gets in terms of administrative responsibility, the further removed he or she is, of necessity, from what's taking place on the firing line. These individuals often do not need to know and may not even understand the detail level. The state of the art could have moved beyond them. Certainly, they rarely have time to wade through a tedious presentation of technicality.

The standard approach in this instance has been to shoot for the median level—the person in the middle. In my experience, all this does is frustrate the most important readers, those making management decisions and those ultimately doing the job.

Consider how each level is actually going to use what I write. What does the person at the top need? He or she probably wants a summary or overview. We know the people on the firing line need specifics. I still only want to write one memorandum, so I must structure my content to make it easily used in both instances.

Why not begin my memo with a summary, either in introductory paragraphs or as a cover memo? This overview would be followed by detailed information, perhaps in the form of an attached report. Now I've touched all the bases.

The individual at the highest level of administrative authority need only read the summary. That should meet his or her administrative requirements for general information. Of course, if he or she wishes to review the detail, it's there.

The individuals on the firing line have the detail they need to do the job, but they also have access to something I consider equally important—the understanding of the situation now held (through the overview) by the people they work for. How often, in data processing areas, does management's viewpoint of a project or service vary considerably from the outlook of the employees directly involved? Not here. My document should be easily utilized by all my readers, in spite of their diverse needs. It also should ensure consistent interpretation of the available facts through all levels of administrative responsibility.

4
Key II—
The Think-Through

This second list of organizational techniques applies directly to response situations. It is invaluable when, rather than initiating a channel of communication, we are replying to a letter, memorandum, or report someone sent to us.

Again, as with MAKING VALID ASSUMPTIONS, THE THINK-THROUGH is usually completed prior to the actual writing process.

A. Go over each letter, memo, or report just before you answer it.

Say something comes in across my desk. I read it. I know I must reply, but I'm busy at the moment. I'm on the phone. Someone is at my desk. I have to go to lunch. There may be an interval of several hours before I actually put pen to paper. Finally, I sit down, take out the memo or letter I received, and start to write. I don't reread, do I? I rely on my photographic memory—the one I don't have.

That interval of time between reading and responding accounts for a great deal of misunderstanding in written communication.

We must learn to read anything we plan to reply to *at the time* we start to write. I go one step further. I underline anything in the original document that is a clue to me as to my reader's expectations. I also make one or two word notations in the margin—information I must supply, points to be stressed. If you do this, you will have the skeleton of your response right in front of you. Even more important, your outlined reply will be as closely related as possible to what your reader sent to you.

B. Find out what's been done before.

This is a necessity partially because of the size of most data processing environments and partially because of the so-called team concept. Other individuals in your area are probably working on a different segment of the same assignment as you, and they're dealing with the same people. This can create confusion. Too often, previous correspondence documenting a situation becomes diffused—say between analysts in one group and programmers in another—leaving even co-workers uninformed.

As a result, I'm seeing conflicting decisions on the same subject go from a data processing area out to a user or support department. What impression does this create of our competency and analytical judgment? Even worse than appearing totally disorganized, we now must leave the option as to which decision to accept up to our reader. Do they ever select the one we prefer?

Also, I've seen differing explanations for a problem sent from a data processing department to the same reader. Imagine what this does for our credibility and what it says about our capability to correct the original problem.

Check around. Take time before writing anything to bring yourself up to date. Make sure you are beginning your communication where you should be.

In large organizations, where documents are often scattered—one file here, another at a different location—the only practical solution is a READING FILE. This is set up on a centrally located desk or table and contains copies of all written communication in chronological sequence, divided sensibly. The file categories may vary from department to department, even within the same organization. For example, some use project designation or system name, others the names of individual respondents.

Arrange your READING FILE under headings based on your area's task identification. It should only take seconds for people in your department to flip through and put themselves in the know—prior to embarrassing and costly duplication of effort.

C. Get your objective firmly in mind.

In MAKING VALID ASSUMPTIONS, we decided it was always the writer's responsibility to define the "what." If we are now just replying, most people would say the individual writing us has already defined the objective. I disagree.

How many times do we deal with people who don't know enough to ask the right questions? How often do we deal with people who don't know enough to ask for what they really need?

In data processing, this is commonplace. It puts responsibility back on us. Whether we are opening a line of communication or responding to one established by someone else, *we* define objective. In fact, we often must be willing to go beyond what people asked for and provide them—based on our greater experience and technical expertise—with what they actually require.

This takes tact, doesn't it? We can't respond, saying, "Look dummy . . . ." We must introduce our definition of what is important and necessary through the suggestion mode.

"Have you considered . . . ?"
"Perhaps you might . . . ."
"Would . . . work?"

Suggestion mode implies that final option rests with the reader. Be aware it doesn't. Our response has simply been structured to perform an educational function, showing our reader alternatives he or she may not even have known existed—alternatives we recognize as better for the reader than the original request.

D. Put together a convincing message.

I'm convinced that sequence—the way in which we organize content on a page—is as important, if not more important, than what we say.

Any number of sequence formats are available. Select the one best suited to your objective prior to writing and you should avoid frustrating reorganization of first, second, even third drafts.

Let's examine some sequence formats. One of the most familiar—although not the most effective—is associated with the Status Report. Status Reports are most frequently written in chronological sequence—where I've been, where I am, where I'm going.

One of the newer formats, especially geared to readers with low levels of technical comprehension, is simplest idea to most complex. As your reader understands your first and least complicated idea, he or she has a building block on which to move to comprehension of your next and more complicated idea. In effect, you are moving your reader through the same mental process in understanding your idea that you went through in developing it in the first place.

Perhaps the most prevalent sequence format in business communication is that of priorities. We put what is most important first. But most important to whom—to us or to the reader? The temptation, of course, is to put what is most important to us first. We defined objective. We want our concerns right up front. This does not work. If I'm your reader and you put what is most important to you first, I'll start skimming through, looking for the answers to my mental questions and concerns. Then I'll probably call you with a stupid question you answered in your first paragraph. Skimmers don't go back and reread. In order to get and hold reader interest, put what is most important to your reader first. Once you have his or her full attention, you'll get your turn.

This is like the old "I've got some bad news and I've got some good news"—which comes first? I hope you didn't think "the good," but you might have. We've taught people for years, in every type of management training, to always say something nice, then cut people off at the knees.

The best example of this is "erasure words"—which data processors badly abuse, by the way. What's an "erasure word"? Well, suppose I came to you and said, "You're doing a great job . . . *but* . . . ." Swish! I just erased my first phrase, and I'm in a much worse position than if I had never said it. Now the entire time I tell you what's wrong, you're thinking to yourself, "If I'm doing such a great job, what's all this garbage she's handing me?"

Here's another. I say to you, "That's a fantastic idea . . . *however* . . . ." Swish! I did it again. Now while I list my reservations about your suggestion, you're thinking, "What is this? She just said my idea was fantastic."

Bad news first. No exceptions.

If you follow this format, at least you are walking out on the most positive note possible. Also, the reason something is bad news is often that it is a negative response to what is most important to your reader. Why take a chance on his or her skimming down looking for it, only to miss your good news altogether.

Make "erasure words" work for you. Reverse them. Bad news first lets you interject motivation into an otherwise negative atmosphere.

For example, I would come to you and say: "I'm having some problems with your area. Problem A. Problem B. Problem C. *However,* I think you're doing a great job with a difficult situation." Now who's motivated to at least try to correct problems A, B, and C?

I can say to you: "I see some problems with your idea. Problem X. Problem Y. Problem Z. *However,* in general, I think it's a solid suggestion and I think we should try it." Who now will kill themselves to correct Problems X, Y, and Z? I think you will. In many such situations, I had better get some motivation in there, because who is probably the only one who can correct Problems X, Y, and Z?

Notice the content remains the same. It's the sequence that makes the difference.

E. Decide on approach. Tone can be as important as content.

People consistently say to me: "Randi, we are all businessmen and women here. We're professionals, and the way someone feels about a situation has nothing whatsoever to do with what goes on."

That's wrong.

Individuals in any organization feel as well as think. They do read between the lines. Have you ever sent out what you felt was a rational, businesslike document and then been appalled at the violence of your reader's reaction? That, strictly, is a function of tone.

Here's how it happens. Suppose I write to Tom Murphy with a complaint. I don't like what I'm getting from his area, and I make my dissatisfaction clear. Tom is a businessman, a data processing professional. He sits down and writes me a sensible and, to him, reasonable explanation of the problem. Of course, the entire time he's writing this business masterpiece, he's thinking to himself: "That stupid broad. If she knew her job, if her people knew their jobs, this would never have happened. She comes down here with one more complaint and I'm going to slit her throat.'' Now Tom would never put those sentiments on paper. What, however, are the odds of my reading them between the lines? 95%? 100%? If I was angry before, I am now going straight up the wall and probably up one administrative level in Tom's department.

Tone is highly contagious. If you appear angry, frustrated, impatient in your written communication, you have given your reader permission to react in exactly the same way—or worse. As tempting as it is sometimes (and no one knows better than I just how tempting it can be), don't buy ten seconds worth of self-satisfaction by being sarcastic or facetious, only to create a communication gap that will plague you the rest of your professional life. Go out. Frighten children and small dogs on the street. Kick the soda machine. Do whatever is necessary to get your head on straight. Then come back and write. No one expects you to come on like Pollyanna in a touchy situation. Just stay service-oriented and courteous in tone. It works.

F. Bounce your idea off someone else.

This is standard communications theory, and you have probably heard it before. Some people discuss their ideas prior to writing. Others share a first draft. Of course, we wouldn't do it with everything we write, but I do find this approach occasionally valuable in data processing for two reasons:

1. Many of us are closely involved day after day with technical detail. This can make it difficult, if not impossible, to step back and provide a comprehensive overview in certain situations. It's the old ''can't see the forest for the trees.'' Here, another individual's perspective can point the way to elements of content, crucial to our reader, that we might have omitted because they are obvious to us.

2. Tone. We discussed the importance of proper approach in written communication. I personally, however, find it incredibly difficult to discern my own tone. I hear, in what I write, the attitude I expect to hear. If this is true for you also, I suggest asking someone to scan your document, not for content or sequence, but for sound.

I mentioned bouncing ideas off someone else in one seminar I conducted, and a man said he had this technique down pat. He simply selected the stupidest person he knew and presented his data, figuring if he or she understood it—anyone would understand it.

This is not what I recommend. For one thing, if that person ever found out why he or she was selected, the communication channel between the two of you would permanently die. Choose someone from your area who at least has some knowledge of your subject (and your reader, if possible) and ask that person to offer you his or her analysis of content, and interpretation of tone.

G. Set your plan aside.

This is the only cure I'm aware of for Writer's Block—that horrible experience of having your material in your head, but being totally incapable of getting it down on paper.

When this happens, stop. Go do something else. Don't get a drink of water or look out a window. You'll still be hassling mentally. Take action that requires your full attention and forces you to think of something else. When you return to your original writing task, you should have a fresh perspective.

There are severe time restrictions associated with this suggestion. You cannot productively defer any writing more than morning to afternoon, afternoon to the next morning. I have learned, through bitter experience, that to set anything aside longer than that is not to break Writer's Block, but to procrastinate about a difficult task you didn't want to do in the first place. I have also learned, again from bitter experience, that the longer you postpone such a task, the more difficult it becomes.

You can also set a document aside after having written it, again with the same time restrictions. Rereading and attempting to edit a communication vehicle immediately after writing it is a total waste. You're too close to your material. Anytime you question content or tone, leave your draft on your desk in the morning or overnight, and read it with a new mental outlook that afternoon or the next morning. This helps catch omissions, errors, or poor approach prior to distribution.

H. Be aware of psychological timing.

This is an area generally ignored in business communication—at great personal cost.

Nationwide surveys confirm that there are better days and worse days on which to communicate in two critical areas:

1. When we are asking someone to do something.
2. When we are asking someone to change the way in which he or she is currently doing something.

All of us are involved in both of these. Certainly, the second is often the more difficult. It's an area where, especially in data processing, experience alerts us to expect reader resistance.

What would you say is the worst possible day? You're right if you think Friday. T.G.I.F.—a cliché, but a true one. I don't know whether people have already mentally checked out for the weekend or what the problem is, but the largest number of negative responses was evoked on Friday.

How about the second worst day? Not surprisingly, it's Monday. Good old blue

Monday. Again, I don't know whether people are hung over or just not geared up for responsive action, but the second largest number of negative responses came in on Monday.

Perhaps the best check on the truth of these surveys is your own reaction. How do you feel when someone lays additional responsibility on you at 3:30 on Friday afternoon? I know what I do. I put it off until Monday—the second worst day. I also have been amazed as I visited organizations in a consulting capacity to note how many staff meetings are regularly scheduled for Friday afternoon or Monday morning, when all are at their absolute worst.

What do you think is the best day? It's Tuesday. The greatest number of positive replies was received first on Tuesday, then Wednesday, then Thursday. Now, I'm not recommending that you time everything you write. That would be ridiculous. Business must be conducted on a timely basis. Besides, it would make no sense to put every corporation in the United States on a three-day work week. We'd turn Tuesday and Thursday into Monday and Friday.

Each of us, however, at one time or another, writes something where an affirmative response from our reader is crucial to *our* success. Here I am suggesting that you time your communication to be received on a Tuesday, Wednesday, or Thursday.

I tested this theory. I prepared a simple memorandum, asking for an administrative decision of no consequence, and distributed it to four departments in four client corporations. The memo was received on Monday. Across the board, in all four departments in all four companies, the answer was no. You know the bit—"Our people are too busy," "We can't get involved this year," etc.

Three weeks later, I sent the same memorandum, same sequence, not one word changed, to the same recipients. It was received on Wednesday. Without exception, the answer this time was yes.

Now this did not surprise me. We've known for years not to buy a car built on a Friday or a Monday. What did surprise me is this. Not one of my respondents had any memory whatsoever of my original memorandum. They had to go to the files to be convinced that the subject had been presented to them before.

I'm sure you get the message. Where an affirmative response is crucial to your success—shoot for a Tuesday, Wednesday, or Thursday.

Psychological timing can apply, on a personal basis, to writing as well as reading. I find everyone has a period during the working day when writing comes more easily and the finished product is better.

Unfortunately, I can't give you any guidelines. The timing or bio-rhythm or whatever is highly personal and each individual must discover his or her own peak performance hours. Mine happen to be morning, so I schedule my time accordingly—organizational and other activities in the P.M., writing in the A.M. Yours may be completely the reverse.

Take several weeks and try varying the times at which you write. Note when you feel most relaxed while writing and when such work goes more quickly. Discovering your most productive writing hours allows you to schedule communication tasks constructively. You write more in a shorter time with less frustration—an advantage anyone in a technical environment can appreciate.

5
Key III—Brevity

Wouldn't you agree that most business communication is incredibly dull? People say letters, memorandums, and reports are boring because the situations discussed are generally not too exciting in the first place. I agree our topics in data processing are often dry, but subject matter alone does not make a document tedious. We've fallen into a pattern of dragging out what we have to say. We go on and *on*, sometimes merely repeating in our last paragraph what we said in our first, using twice the words actually required.

Brevity is a critical criterion in successful business writing. Each word costs money. Lengthy documents are time-consuming and expensive to write, time-consuming and usually frustrating to read. This is not, however, the primary reason I consider brevity so important.

Brevity picks up the tempo. In presenting any material, the ability to get in and get out is highly prized. Eliminate wordiness and you have efficient communication. The writing process is simplified. Reading time is shortened, the reader's attention is held, and a more productive response is encouraged.

A. Don't be "iffy."

"Iffyness" is a common trap. All individuals in data processing fall into it at one time or another.

It usually goes this way. We begin with a ball park statement, a generality. We then spend the rest of our document qualifying our original statement—"should this occur . . ."—"in case of . . ."—"if"—"if"—"if".

One bad aspect of this approach is we provide so much irrelevant detail that our reader loses sight of our basic premise or main idea. He or she gets completely fogged, and is totally unable to distinguish what is important and what is not.

Even worse, we can open a whole can of worms for ourselves by saying too much. Have you ever told someone more than he needed to know—usually about something unpleasant? Now he's worried, isn't he? And, if he's worried, he's going to hassle somebody, usually you. He can't help solve the problem, of course. You must do that—now, however, with someone leaning over your shoulder.

I know why we're "iffy." Again, we've all been burned in the past, and God forbid we should take an unqualified position.

Here's a classic example. It's not in a data processing context, but I think it makes the point. Someone wrote to an insurance company asking the present loan value of his insurance policy. This is a standard inquiry—all insurance companies get this kind of letter, particularly in a down economy. The individual responding to this letter wrote a courteous reply, explaining the present loan value of the insured's policy. Unfortunately, he then went on to explain what would happen if the policyholder were dead *before* he got the letter.

Can you believe it? This just was not information the reader either wanted or needed to know. If he's dead before the letter is delivered, loan information becomes a moot point.

This also was the worst piece of PR I'd ever seen. Doesn't it sound as if the insurance company involved is holding its breath, praying the guy will croak before he can borrow the bread? What a great corporate image!

Let's start imposing some mental discipline. Start with specifics and stay with specifics. Generalities always need at least some qualification.

We can limit ourselves to three major areas of concern. Not all of these will be necessary each time we write, but if we are at least thinking of them, we should touch all the bases for our reader and ourselves—without being "iffy."

The three areas are:

1. *What.* What are you talking about? You've defined objective. Clearly present it to your readers. If they understand *what,* they also know *why.*
2. *When.* Everyone in business is paranoid about dates. Where time framework is involved, spell it out.
3. *How much.* Dollar amount must be plainly expressed. This is not an area some of us are accustomed to considering. Your organization may still be on a funny money rather than an actual money set-up, and cost has not been a crucial factor. More and more corporations, however, are going on cost allocation or charge-back systems—actual dollars—and *how much* is increasingly important.

What, when, and *how much.* Nothing more. Think about it. For instance, I can't believe any of your readers care about *how* you get from Point A to Point B. What they do care about is *what* they're going to get when you arrive at Point B, *when* you're going to get there, and *how much,* if anything, it's going to cost.

Now, I'm a great believer in the management technique of anticipation rather than reaction. This is the ability to forecast or anticipate problems prior to their becoming a crisis, either preventing them altogether or coming up with some way to alleviate them should they occur in spite of our best efforts. Certainly, anticipation is preferable to the brush fire situation prevalent in so many data processing areas.

I am not suggesting you give up anticipation. When, based on your past experience, you can identify legitimate potential problems, of course your reader must be informed. You would only be presenting to your reader, however, those problems that might impact the *what,* the *when,* and the *how much.* If the problems you anticipate are not going to affect these areas, whose problems are they? That's right. They're ours, our internal affair, and no concern of the reader.

B. Eliminate prepositional phrases.

Prepositional phrases are force-of-habit. They're traditional in business writing. We use them because we've always used them. Unfortunately, they are not only wordy, but they make most of our written communication heavy and passive in tone.

Where you can, get rid of them. Make your writing an accurate reflection of the active and competent person you are.

Here are a few common abuses:

"in case of . . ." (if)

Note that except where actually required, we've eliminated the "if" also.

"for the purpose of . . ." (to, for)

"This is for the purpose of informing you . . . ." Of course, you have a purpose. If you didn't you wouldn't be writing in the first place. This phrase always reminds me of the old speaker's technique—tell them what you're going to tell them, tell them, and tell them that you told them. Such phrasing may be effective in a four-hour presentation. Can you imagine how boring it is on one sheet of paper? Don't tell them you're going to tell them. Just do it.

"in reference to . . ." (about)

"This is in reference to your memo of such and such, dated such and such, regarding such and such." Your reader is now skimming or asleep.

Where does any reference to prior communication belong? In a memorandum, we have the Subject heading. In a business letter, we have the Reference line. The

Subject and Reference heading were designed to hold up three full lines of copy. Both are sadly underutilized in most organizations. Think of how much you can lift from the body or context of your document and place in the heading, not even using complete sentences.

I like to see any reference to prior communication by date on the first line, a concise statement of the *what* on the second, and some description of my commitment (for your information, for review and decision) on the third. I now know what went on before, what you're going to talk about, and my personal involvement in your topic—even before I get to your first paragraph. This certainly should buy a more careful reading of your complete text.

"as to . . ." (on, about)

"As to our discussion of . . . ." This is not even proper use of the English language. Any intelligent (and some not so) reader does a double-take when this prepositional phrase appears. Eliminate it altogether, writing "on" or "about" your subject instead.

Another thing I see frequently is a noun sandwiched between two prepositions. This makes any statement dull and ponderous. For example:

"Rocca has two weeks *for analysis of* the report."

This just sits there. It's flat. In no way does it suggest action being taken. We can pick it up by throwing out the prepositional phrase.

"Rocca has two weeks *to analyze* the report."

That's better, but let's make it even stronger. Let's show our reader that action is definitely going to take place.

"Rocca *will analyze* the report within two weeks."

See the difference? Now, our reader knows we are going to do something.

What about references to money? It intrigues me that 90% of the time—when I see dollars and cents mentioned—the phrase "in the amount of" is included.

"A check in the amount of $30 is enclosed."

Of course, the check is in the amount of something. How can money be other than in "the amount of" something? Also, if I send you anything containing dollar amount, where do your eyes go immediately on the page? If you're like me, they go to the money. We *know* it's in "the amount of" something. We only want to know how much.

"Enclosed is a $30 check."

This makes better sense, no pun intended.

If I were you, reading this, I'd be tempted to think: "That's trivia. Prepositional phrases are nothing but trivia, and I'm not going to develop any mental red pencil to get rid of anything that nitpicking." Up until about three years ago, I would have been hard-pressed to argue with you—except to say I dislike prepositional phrases. I think they make what you say colorless and passive in tone. Three years ago, however, professional writers began checking business communication carefully. One area they concentrated on was the prepositional phrase. My colleagues don't like them any better than I do.

The results of this review are staggering.

If you're willing to eliminate this trivia—prepositional phrases—you will eliminate *one-third* of all the words you write in a business context in the course of one year. One-third of all the words you put on paper at your desk are unnecessary prepositions.

Break the prepositional phrase habit. Not only will you be writing one-third fewer words, but your reader will be reading one-third fewer words. What you write will be more direct. It will be better. For those of you who don't like to write, this has to be a good deal.

C. Stick with action verbs.

I am on record that we need more positive statements in business communication. Too many of us sound like we're hedging, even when we're not. Our daily work crunch will become manageable only when our writing conveys recognition of the reader's need for responsive action. A reader who believes we're doing something is a reader off our backs. A reader who senses immediacy in our requests is a reader who replies quickly. Stop substituting nouns for verbs and you create a tone of vigorous commitment.

Traditional format reads this way:

"Please make an adjustment on your testing schedule."

It's an easy matter to introduce your need for prompt action. Jack up the tempo with a more aggressive verb.

"Please *adjust* your testing schedule."

Now, however, we really do it to ourselves. You would probably come to me and say:

"Rändi, please adjust your testing schedule at your earliest convenience."

In any organization, you've just given me the next 15 years.
Or, perhaps, you'd say:

"Rändi, please adjust your testing schedule as soon as possible."

Is my "as soon as possible" ever your "as soon as possible"?

How many times have you written to someone asking, "Please let me have your comments as soon as possible?" When do these comments come in (if at all)? Isn't it usually after you've completed whatever it was you asked your reader to comment on? Now, you not only cannot utilize the comments, but you have alienated your reader by not incorporating his or her viewpoint into your end product.

In data processing, we live with time framework—start date to stop date. We are locked into deadlines. If we must work within a specified time framework, our readers should do the same. The problem has been that no reader can comply with a time restriction he or she knows nothing about.

You know yourself—if anything comes in with "as soon as possible" or "at your earliest convenience," you feel no sense of urgency. Doesn't that document go on the bottom of your "when I have time" pile? If that same request came in containing a definite date, each of us would immediately begin to calculate mentally—rearranging other tasks to fit the time allowed.

Whenever you ask for anything in written communication, ask for it by a specific date, and that date should be several days in advance of when you actually require what you ask for.

For example if you need new scheduling by October 12, you might say:

"Rändi, please adjust your testing schedule by October 10."

Now I understand the time restriction from the beginning.

Suppose I don't adjust my testing schedule by October 10, even though you spelled out time requirements? At least, you are in a position to call me. You still have several days lead time. You aren't going to say, "Listen, stupid, it's the 10th and you're behind." We're always polite in business communication. You'll probably ask, "What's the matter, Rändi? Do you have some questions or problems I can help you with?" Whatever the tone, however, you are going to try to push me, and you can only push successfully when the necessary date was put right out front. You certainly had better not push me if you said, "at your earliest convenience." It simply has not been convenient, and the more you push, the less convenient it becomes.

Here's another familiar example:

"Please give consideration to our cost estimates."

Again, we can interject a sense of required action by changing the verb.

"Please *consider* our cost estimates."

The sentence is immediately stronger. We're in trouble again, though, unless we include a specific date.

Has a user ever waited so long to approve costing figures that by the time you get the sign-off, the costs have gone up? How about finally getting disapproval three weeks after you begin work—allocating people and other expensive resources—on the first phase of the project involved?

Just tacking on a date in this instance, however, might sound pushy. You could be going up several management levels or out to a user and feel uncomfortable with direct pressure like:

"Please consider our cost estimates. Let me hear from you by March 18."

We still must spell out time framework and necessary target dates. We can do it, and not push, by giving reasons. Simply explain why your date must be met.

"Please consider our cost estimates. Let me hear from you by March 18 in order that we may begin March 21."

What are you probably planning to begin March 21? Isn't it usually some development work or data processing service your *reader* wants? You have just given him or her a motive of self-interest for complying with your time constraints. Now your date is the reader's date, and he or she meets it.

I hope you see the importance of action-oriented, positive sentences in evoking reader response. I can't recommend this type of business statement too highly. I do, however, have one caution if you choose to use this approach. Consider this sentence:

"O'Reilley makes omissions in the preparation of time sheets."

I actually saw something like this in a memorandum I reviewed. It is a positive statement. I wonder, about its effectiveness, however. If you were the reader, would it leave any questions unanswered in your mind? I know it did in mine. How many omissions? What kind? How often? There's a great deal of difference between forgetting to dot your i's and cross your t's, and deliberately fudging time allocation. Of which is O'Reilly guilty? We don't know, and no matter which we select, are we likely to be correct? I doubt it, probably to the detriment of poor O'Reilly.

Write positive sentences. Use action verbs and include dates. Just be sure no direct statement you make is open to any interpretation other than the one you originally intended. Our example is a generality. In presenting definitive information, we must, again stay with specifics.

D. Watch out for "who," "which," and "that" phrases.

These phrases are also largely force-of-business-habit. Most of them are over-worked—I've seen one-page memos containing 14 "that" phrases—and many of them are unnecessary. Eliminate all you can.

For instance:

"The proposal which is enclosed" is, of course, the "enclosed proposal."
"Barnes, (who is) our agent in Hartford . . . ." The "who is" phrase is totally superfluous.
"New procedures that save time" are "timesaving procedures."

And here is the garbage phrase of the western world: "Any information that will be helpful will be appreciated at your earliest convenience." You're talking about "helpful information" and remember it will not be helpful unless you receive it by a specific date.

These phrases can be dangerous. The average reader can absorb just so much on the page—physically and mentally—and then he or she takes a break. Physically, we blink. No one can focus on typed words for too long. Mentally, we actually shift gears, interrupting concentration. Include a "who," "which," or "that" phrase and you trigger this physical and mental hiatus about 80% of the time. Unfortunately, we generally use these phrases to modify our most important ideas and wind up breaking reader comprehension at exactly the point we can least afford to do so.

E. Say good-bye to "very" and "real."

Eliminate these adverbs from your written vocabulary. They have been misused to an extent where true meaning has been obscured, if not altogether lost.

I tested these words. I gave three memorandums, each containing "very" and "real," to a selected group of readers. Once they had reviewed the memos, I asked, "Do these memorandums contain the words 'very' and 'real'?" *Sixty percent* of my respondents said no. "Very" and "real" have been carelessly thrown into so many business documents that 60% of your readers don't even see them. So why write them?

Even worse was the reaction of the remaining 40%. They said, "Yes, these documents do contain the words 'very' and 'real'." I then asked them, "How do you feel about content, about what was presented?" Over half replied, "It's a put-on," or "He doesn't mean it."

If you want someone to doubt your sincerity—and few of us can afford that in a business context—use or misuse one of these words. Take these examples:

"We are *very* optimistic . . . ."

Most users automatically add six months to a year. Believe it or not, "We are optimistic . . ." is a more convincing statement.

"You have done us a *real* favor in bringing this to our attention."

Is this as opposed to an "unreal" favor? I am not sure how the word "real" crept into our business vocabularies, but I don't like it. They probably haven't done us a favor at all. They've just dumped in our laps the biggest problem of our careers. We know it and they know it; yet, here we come, tripping like Pollyanna with the "you have done us a real favor" bit.

"Real," more than any other word, is also a tip-off that an erasure word is on the way. I recently received a letter beginning, "Rändi, it is always a real pleasure to have you with us . . . ." What did I know was coming? "However . . . ."

Another example of "real" creating problems, particularly in the communication between data processors and other areas, is our insistence on using the phrase "real world" to underscore the feasibility of our technical hypotheses. If you wish to alienate someone, simply suggest that you (and only you) live in the "real world," implying your respondent has spent all of his or her professional life in Disneyland. The way in which anyone perceives his working environment is, to that individual, the "real" world. Our job is to understand that perception and deal with it, not discount it.

F. Don't be redundant.

Some people collect stamps. I collect garbage phrases because I'm surrounded by them constantly. Like others we've discussed, these phrases are primarily force-of-habit. Here are some you may recongize:

Advance planning

Planning, by definition, must be done when? In advance, or it's not planning. Whenever anyone says to me, "Advance planning indicates . . . ," I know he or she iş talking from hindsight. If not, why the great effort to assure me he or she anticipated the situation in "advance"? I recognize a legitimate distinction between long-range planning and short-range planning, but "advance planning" is garbage, pure and simple.

By the way, I made this positive declaration in one seminar I conducted and a man said he was sorry to hear it, as he was from the *Advance Planning Department*. Can you imagine coming in each morning and showing yourself at a desk under a sign reading "advance planning"? That's how much such foolishness has permeated our business language.

Return back

"Please return back the enclosed form." If someone is going to return anything, where must it come? It must come back.

This phrase also is not even proper English. I find most readers do a double-take when they see it. They then begin to doubt the intelligence of the person who wrote it.

Arrange to inform

This phrase is dangerous on both sides of the communication channel. Suppose I write to you and say, "I will arrange to inform you . . . ." Based on past episodes, what do you know? The next person you hear from will *not* be me. I don't want any part of you or your problem, and I have already begun the delegate-responsibility, pass-the-buck routine. If I were going to help you, I would either provide the required information or tell you the date on which you could expect it.

It's even worse the other way. I write to you, saying, "Please arrange to inform me . . . ." By implication, what am I saying? Isn't it, "You don't know, but, please God, find someone in your area who does, and let him or her get back to me"? If I thought I could get an adequate response from you, I would just ask my questions and wait for you to reply.

Basic fundamentals

A large computer corporation (who shall remain nameless) did this to us. Fundamentals, however, by definition, *are* basic. We can refer to the "fundamentals" of something, the "basics" of something else, but we cannot refer to the "basic fundamentals" of anything.

Some data processors have gotten more sophisticated and speak of "fundamental principles." The problem is the same. "Principles" are principles because they are "fundamental." "Fundamental principles" is just one more redundant junk-phrase.

Carbon copy

This is one of my favorites. I receive a letter stating, "Enclosed is a carbon copy." I look. It's a Dennison. It's a Pitney-Bowes. It's a Xerox. It probably is not a carbon copy because, where they can avoid them, large organizations do not use carbons. They're expensive and they're messy. My initial reaction is some idiot put the wrong thing in the envelope. I don't have a carbon of anything.

The word is "copy." Who cares what kind? In fact, secretarial manuals published recently have completely eliminated the "cc:" designation from the bottom of business documents. They go "c:" for copy or "info. c:" for informational copy, because that's what it is. Perhaps you thought ''cc:'' stood for complimentary copy? It didn't. It was ''carbon copy'' and is no longer accurate.

(Distinctly) Unique

''Unique'' is a popular word in data processing. Have you ever noticed how many of our problems, if not their solutions, are ''unique''? It's a great word, and I'm happy for you to use it, as long as you know what it means. ''Unique,'' by definition, means different from anything else. Because of this, the word ''unique'' cannot be modified.

For example, nothing can be ''distinctly unique.'' It is either ''distinct'' or ''unique.'' Also, something cannot be ''very unique,'' as nothing is ''uniquer'' than something else. Above all, nothing you describe can be ''somewhat unique.'' That is like saying someone is ''somewhat pregnant.'' One either is pregnant or one is not—something is either unique or it isn't. Just keep that rule of thumb in mind.

In my travels, I find my list of garbage words and phrases growing, with the same ones becoming popular simultaneously in all areas of the country. ''Consensus of opinion'' is one example. Consensus, of course, means agreement among once varying opinions, so consensus ''of opinion'' is redundant. All that is necessary is the one word. ''The consensus is . . . .''

Another abuse is ''irregardless.'' This is not a word in the English language—I hope you realize that. Some dictionaries, recently published, do contain the word. Their definition is succinctly stated as ''nonword.'' I would hesitate to use ''irregardless,'' based on that definition. The proper word is ''regardless.''

Start examining what you write. In data processing, we're overconfident of our ability to get away with careless word usage. ''Input'' is a good example. We sold ''input'' to the extent that the original definition of data going person to machine disappeared. Individuals now ''input'' to other individuals, committees ''input'' to management groups—the word is universally misapplied.

We are not succeeding as well, however, with others—some we discussed and some I'm sure you know without discussion. Use words without conscious thought, and you may unwittingly paint for your reader a disastrous picture of your personal ability.

G. Start without "it is" and "there is."

These introductory phrases can force us to be passive, almost weary, in tone. Again, I know why we use them even when they're not necessary. Often, we have our thoughts together mentally, but nothing is coming out in writing. So, we begin ''it is'' or ''there is.'' Now, we've broken the barrier. We can, at least, put something on paper. Not something good, usually, but something.

Here's a simple technique to change this approach. Look at this sentence:

"It is a sign of good planning when cost estimates are accurate."

Work with it. Take what you, as the writer, consider to be most important about the thought you wish to express and put it *first* in the sentence. This way it receives the greatest amount of play. Your reader is able to identify with it immediately.

Only you can decide. In our example, we have at least two choices. We could emphasize "good planning." We could be most concerned with "accurate cost estimates." I would select "accurate cost estimates" and rewrite the statement this way:

"Accurate cost estimates are a sign of good planning."

My version is shorter, a great advantage, and also stronger and more concise. Yet, all I did was put what was most important to me first.

What about the quality of motivation? Difficult to interject into any business writing, motivation is never introduced with a blasé, listless "it is" or "there is" opening.

Consider this:

"There is a certain format to be observed in preparing status reports."

Sound familiar? Would you even read the entire sentence—say, in a procedures manual—or would you begin skimming?

Let's apply our technique. What is most important to you, as the writer, in that sentence? Perhaps it's the format itself. We could say:

"A certain format is to be observed in preparing status reports."

This still sounds stilted to me. I feel the observation, or the way my respondent fills out the form, is what's crucial. I would begin:

"Please observe this format in preparing status reports."

Do you see the difference in motivational impact between the original statement and mine? They can't be compared. Yet, again, all I did was identify the element most pertinent to my objective and put it *first* in the sentence.

H. Give up "business" language.

We're confronted daily with a separate business language—"businessese," I call it—that cripples any exchange of information or ideas. Let's examine some of these "we've always done it this way" sacred cows. If they're not buying us anything—or worse, if they're creating problems—let's eliminate them altogether or find acceptable alternatives.

Don't quote me.

Suppose I walked in, sat down across from you at your desk, and you said: "Good morning, Rändi. Nice day, isn't it?" I then replied: "Good morning, Rändi. Nice day, isn't it? Yes, it certainly is." What would you think? Wouldn't you think I was eccentric, at the least? After all, I'm repeating everything you say to me before I answer you.

None of us would do this in a verbal context. We know we'd sound absurd. But how many of us spend 25 minutes or more of our valuable time, attempting to paraphrase in our first paragraph what someone said to us in his letter or memorandum? Same approach, isn't it? Our reader immediately begins skimming, thinking, "I know that." Even worse than eliciting only cursory reader attention, this repetition can create misunderstanding and reader resistance. Here are two good reasons:

One, paraphrasing is the most difficult form of writing. Unless you trained at *Reader's Digest,* I doubt you're good at it. Inevitably, something important is omitted or misconstrued.

Two, paraphrasing in business situations, no matter how well done, has to fail. In effect I would be taking your writing, putting it in my words, and sending it back to you. Whose version are you bound to prefer?

Now I know there are times when our reader must know exactly what he or she initially wrote in order to use what we are now saying. There are ways to ensure this without nonproductive paraphrasing, however.

First, where does any reference to prior communication belong? Remember, we record it by date in the Subject heading of a memo or the Reference line in a business letter. Let your reader review his or her own copy.

Should you suspect your reader won't get up and go to the file—readers think, "I remember what I said," when they usually don't—here's a second option. Enclose a copy of your respondent's original document. Now the reader can put his or her copy side by side with yours. No misunderstanding is possible. Also, it should interest you to know that including a copy is generally cheaper for your organization than your investment of time in attempting to paraphrase.

Do not, however, throw it away by saying in the first sentence of your letter or memo, "Enclosed is a copy of yours of the . . . ." If you do, most readers won't even look at it. Just include a copy without mentioning it. Now, in order to find out what it is, they must read it.

With this second technique, some readers may be offended. They suspect you're thinking exactly what you are thinking—that they don't know what they said. If you feel a reader may react negatively, simply put "c:" and someone's name (usually your boss's) at the conclusion of your response. Now you have an acceptable reason for enclosing a copy of your respondent's letter or memorandum as the individual referenced did not see the original.

A third option also exists, although rarely used except in reply to specific questions. You are allowed to quote directly—not paraphrase—up to four lines from your respondent's document. The lines must be enclosed in quotation marks and set up as a separate paragraph, isolated by white space. With this method, you can restate your reader's questions or comment, then present your response.

"We are in receipt of . . . ."

This is superfluous overkill. If you were not "in the receipt of" your reader's letter or memorandum, what could you not do?

"As I understand . . . ."

I tested this phrase. After showing readers memos beginning this way, I asked their interpretation. Without fail, each said, "He (the writer) doesn't understand." They're correct, aren't they? Don't we use this phrase most frequently when we either don't understand or are unsure?

If you do not understand, ask. Spell out the additional information required or ask for clairification. No reader can pinpoint exactly what's incorrect in an "as I understand" paragraph. Inevitably, he or she misses something. I see one memo beginning, "As I understand . . . ." The reply to that begins, "As I understood . . . ." Yet a third memo (same subject) opens with, "I had understood . . . ." All either party knows for sure is that they are definitely *not* on the same wavelength.

If you do understand, why rehash? Just state the action taken or decision reached based on your understanding. Should you be wrong, your respondent will be on the phone 10 seconds after receiving your communication to let you know.

"As you know . . . ."

This is insulting. If I already know, don't waste your time or mine with a repeat performance. What we are actually saying to our reader with this opening is, "You don't know, but you should," and anyone receiving it goes immediately on the defensive. If you honestly don't think your reader knows, or aren't sure, simply state your information with no implication of reader ignorance.

The "as you know" phrase is also increasingly used in large organizations to turn rumor into accepted dogma. People out politicking always preface their half-truths and innuendoes with "as you know," making their readers embarrassed to admit they don't.

Don't reiterate instructions.

All too often, the instructions we present to our readers are available somewhere else. They're printed on a form or spelled out in something like a procedures manual. When we repeat instructions—those obtainable somewhere else—in the body of our memo or letter, where does our reader read them? In our document. Where does he or she not read them? On the form or in the manual, unfortunately. So, anytime our readers encounter a similar situation in the future, they're going to come to us to find out what to do. Some data processors spend the bulk of their professional lives answering just such stupid questions.

Respond to these inquiries by referring your reader to the original source. Say, "See manual 10, page 3, paragraph 8," or "See instructions, form #32456." This performs an educational function, as well as providing an answer. Your reader now knows where to go for guidelines, without asking you. Any questions about method or instructions you do receive should be those exceptions to the established rule where your expert judgment is actually required.

Don't advise or inform.

We advise or inform in everything we write. The trick is not to appear arbitrary or arrogant doing so. Don't open any communication with "This is to advise you" or "This is to inform you." Simply state the necessary information. Readers *know* they're being informed or advised.

"It will be appreciated . . . ."

"It will be appreciated if you will let me hear from you at your earliest convenience." How often have you seen that sentence? We use it increasingly in memorandums. With the traditional business letter, we had "Sincerely Yours" or its equivalent to get us out. In memos, we don't. All of us are conditioned to be polite, and it can appear curt to us just to say what we must and sign our name. Hence the garbage phrase closing to soften our exit.

Here's a two-word, one-sentence paragraph to much more effectively end any memorandum:

"Thank you."

Granted, it's a cliché, but it's a shorter cliché, than the "it will be appreciated . . . " number and far more natural. We say "thank you" almost without thought. Even when handing a salesclerk *our* money, what do we usually say? You can be thanking your respondent for nothing more than reading your document—and with some I read, the "thank you" should be in all caps.

"If you have any questions or need additional information, please feel free to contact me."

I'm a Virginian, and in Virginia we have an expression, "Y'all drop by." Of course, if you did, we'd drop dead. It's just an expression—a way of saying good-bye.

I feel the same way about the "if you have any questions or need additional information, please feel free to contact me" phrase as I do about "Y'all drop by." Most of the time, we don't mean it. God forbid our readers should call with problems. If you aren't looking for a response, don't ask for one. That's empty courtesy. Just say, "Thank you," and get out.

When you do hope to actively evoke response from your reader, tighten up the request. For example, we never tell anyone in business to "feel free." That conjures up butterflies and flower-filled meadows. Also, if we want any reader to take our open-door policy seriously, we must include our telephone number. Where telephone number appears, I or any other reader has direct access to you as a person. I don't have to look you up in an internal telephone directory. I don't have to call into your organization from outside and be passed telephone extension to telephone extension trying to find you. We all know how frustrating that routine is. Be direct.

"If I can help you further, please call me at ext. 764."

Now your readers know you mean it. They can reach for the telephone as soon as they finish reading—while content and questions are still fresh and the communication channel is wide open.

6
Key IV—
Word Selection

This Key is a natural companion to the Key of BREVITY. Intelligent word selection refines our vocabularies, making material presented to a reader brief and easily understood.

Choose words whose meaning and impact will foster your objective in writing. Knowing how you define words and your reaction to your interpretation is important. Anticipating your reader's comprehension and his possible emotional response to his definition is equally crucial.

A. Enlist the mind's eye of your reader.

This technique is included because many of us in data processing must sell concept—our idea of the way something should be done. Good writing is usually not difficult when we have something specific to depict. It becomes a formidable task, however, when we must convincingly explain our opinions or observations.

Here's an example. Say I have a tire. I can write: "This tire is 52 inches high. It has 3 inches of tread." I can be explicit. I can be brief. You understand exactly what I am describing.

It's a whole different ball game with ideas. Therories rarely provide concrete objects to describe. Concept is often the writer's personal viewpoint, easily misconstrued by any reader. Unless we remember this. All human beings think in terms of *visual* images. That's the way the human brain operates. I've been discussing effective written communication with you—my opinion of how it should work. Yet I'd be willing to bet the whole time I've been presenting theory, you've had a film running in your mind. You're actually seeing mental pictures of documents you've written or read, people you've dealt with, situations common to your working environment.

Make this biological and psychological fact work for you in your writing.

Whenever you must sell concept, take a piece of scrap paper and without worrying about spelling or sequence, write down what you see in your head when you think about your idea. Record your specific, concrete images. Each individual in data processing visualizes different elements depending on job responsibility and the situation being discussed. Some see a particular hardware configuration, others a definitive output format. Some visualize user environment or the data to be interpreted. Whatever *you* see, write it down.

Once you have this list of well-constructed images, it's not hard to work from it to a concise business document, easily understood by your reader. What you now write encourages your reader to go through the same mental process in grasping your ideas that you went through in developing them in the first place. You are allowing him to visualize your ideas in exactly the same way you do. I know of no way two people can be more on the same wavelength than that.

This is why in the English language, we say, "I see," when we really mean, "I understand."

B. Be specific.

We discussed being specific and its importance to BREVITY. Now, I would like you to see its relationship to proper and effective word selection.

We all tend to use additional and unnecessarily complicated words the minute we put something on paper. Somehow, we've been taught our writing should be a monument to our intelligence, a showcase for our extensive vocabularies. Actually, such word usage is confusing, making it tough for any reader to get the gist of what we're saying with a first reading.

Take this example:

"If you would care to forward your Data Processing Services Request with attached form #7060, we will endeavor to expedite return of the aforementioned Confirmation Memo."

Did you get that? I certainly didn't. There are some goodies in there— "aforementioned," "expedite." Were you impressed? I doubt it. In spite of the big words and fancy business phrasing, the sentence bombs. It sounds stilted—a bad impression for any writer to create. Even worse, it's hard to understand with one reading and few of us are ever happy about having to reread.

Try this version:

"We will send out a Confirmation Memo within a week of receiving your Data Processing Services Request with attached form #7060."

This is immediately understandable. This sequence is also better psychological organization. We should always tell our reader what we will do for him before telling him what he must do for us. Utilize the KISS principle—KEEP IT SIM-PLE, STUPID. No one is impressed with sophisticated language if it retards comprehension.

The ability to motivate is also dependent on specific word usage. As we've just seen, improper word selection hinders understanding. What is your instinctive reaction to something you don't understand? Is it positive or negative? With most of us, the reaction is negative. Certainly, we reason, if an idea were any good, *we* would understand it. No reader ever picks up writer conviction or enthusiasm from a cloudy presentation.

As illustration, we could use any number of phrases popular in contemporary America. These phrases immediately convey the positive attributes conducive to motivation and acceptance. Take a look at the forerunner of one of these phrases:

"More political clout to the downtrodden and oppressed minorities."

Can you identify its more popular version?

That's right—"Power to the People!"—and I think you can see how much more difficult the first version would be to yell at rallies.

Many of us have the ability to manipulate language. We can elect to come on like an economics professor. If you choose to consistently employ your extensive vocabulary in your business writing however, do not be surprised when you fail to motivate anyone. Empty rhetoric is always a dead end.

We all know what happens to any memorandum or report chock full of $65 words. Everyone reading it thinks: "Wow, this writer is certainly intelligent. This is incredible. What a great job." We all also know what then happens as a result of this marvelous document—*nothing*. People must understand to act. No one is going to accept or implement anything if he must admit ignorance in the process.

Here's one last example of the power of carefully selected words to convey meaning and enthusiasm. I found this sentence in a memo I reviewed:

"Mr. Jones displays the finest part of management and technical skills relating to the above job description."

Poor Mr. Jones. His abilities are already stereotyped at the level of corporate BS. How much more human and convincing to say:

"Mr. Jones is right for the job. I hired him."

C. Control reader concentration.

The arrangement of the words you select also affects comprehension. We can structure our content to set the physical pace, moving our reader from thought to thought at a rate conducive to better understanding. In fact, by placing words properly, we can actually create pauses on paper. Pauses that allow our readers to clear the decks mentally as they read, much as they would listening to us in a verbal context.

My example of this is highly simplistic. The technique demonstrated, however, will work no matter how complex or technical your material may be. Consider this:

"Your presentation was enjoyed by Ms. Johnson, who directed that your list of recommendations be implemented by all departments."

The writer of that sentence has made valid assumptions about his reader. If you make a presentation, what's the first thing you want to know? Isn't it, "How did it go over?" Certainly, if you offered something in the context of your presentation, your second mental question would be "Are they going to use it?"

We can accurately anticipate our reader's concerns and questions in many business situations. Why not answer them directly and in the *reader's* mental sequence:

"Ms. Johnson enjoyed your presentation."

First question answered directly. Obviously, Ms. Johnson is the primary concern of our reader, or she wouldn't need to be mentioned by name. We therefore put her first in our sentence structure, clearly expressing her reaction in brief format. Our reader now shifts gears mentally, moving naturally to his second concern:

"She directed all departments to implement your plan."

Again, a concise response, in the reader's frame of reference.

In effect, through our word and content placement, we are walking our reader through our material step by step in a manner as closely related as possible to his already established question. Its immediate answer in our document provides the "pause" or mental transition so vital to understanding and acceptance.

Try this approach the next time you must communicate with a reader whose data processing knowledge is minimal. I find this technique invaluable with long, interpretative documents like a Feasibility Study or a Management Proposal. Where arrangement of material effectively controls reader concentration, comprehension and acceptance levels go right through the roof.

D. Acknowledge your reader.

We defined communication as interaction between people. Any such interaction is impossible, of course, without written acknowledgment of our reader's individuality. Only by affording such personal recognition, can we encourage others to acknowledge us as individuals also. No one functions well as just one more cog in an anonymous machine.

Interdependency is often a fact of business life. Because of this, the new formats and more modern word usage now surfacing in business communication encourage reader identification. They attempt to provide guidelines for cultivating mutual respect and recriprocity in action. The most recent techniques spring directly from the increasing popularity of a personalized approach in business writing. Some work well. Others are abused, preventing the profitable dialogue between individuals a more personal tone should create.

Let's take a look.

1. Address your reader by name.

Many organizations in the United States—with more jumping on the bandwagon daily—have eliminated the formal salutation altogether from their business letters. They no longer begin "Dear Mr. Johnson:" but drop immediately into their first paragraph with "Thank you, Mr. Johnson, for contacting us . . . " or something similar. The obvious intent is to personalize through informal reader recognition.

I'd say this trend is here to stay. Each of us should begin to use our reader's name in the body or context of our letters, memorandums, or reports, where appropriate. Unfortunately, this technique is easily overdone. For example, have you ever received one of those awful advertisements that repeats and repeats and *repeats* your name:

> "Congratulations, *Mrs. Smith.* You have been selected from 6,000 subscribers, *Mrs. Smith,* to have a chance at our big prize. Just think, *Mrs. Smith,* you and all the *Smiths* could win the *Smith's* dream vacation . . . . "

By the fifth mention of my name in such a letter (if I'm still reading), I'm ready to throw up—literally. Any sense of personal interaction is destroyed by the "unnaturalness" of repetition. We need ground rules limiting use of reader name to sensible numbers and placement. After all, effective personalization must be unaffected in tone.

Take the role of the reader for a minute. If I send you anything containing your name, don't your eyes automatically go to your name, wherever it is located on the page? Our name attracts us, almost as if it were printed in italics. Also, if I ask you what you remember about what I said, won't you immediately recall the statement prefaced by your name? Any content is accentuated by a personal reference to reader identity.

Knowing how we react to our names helps us formulate guidelines for effective use of our reader's name:

A. If you have one major idea you wish your reader to identify with and remember, preface that statement with his or her name.

B. When presenting a multiplicity of ideas, relatively equal in importance, use reader name in your first sentence. It's an immediate attention-getter and should ensure a careful reading.

C. In informal situations, placing the reader's name in our closing sentence creates a relaxed and friendly exit.

D. Certainly, we would only employ reader name once in any one-page business document, twice as an absolute maximum in anything longer.

Two cautions:

One, familiarity is a factor. Your reader's first name is only appropriate if you know him or her well enough to use it with confidence.

Two, there is an increasing tendency on the part of business writers to preface the one statement they know the reader will not like with his or her name. Acknowledgment here becomes a sandbag technique, rarely successful, and resented by readers in decision-making or administrative roles. No one likes to feel pressured, even subtly. Familiarity should establish close working relationships, not breed contempt.

2. Congratulate where appropriate.

How long has it been since you wrote a brief letter or memorandum saying "thanks" to someone who took time out of a busy day to do something for you? He could have provided information, taken action, made a fast decision—whatever. I hope it hasn't been long. Too many of us deal repeatedly with the same people, never acknowledging their efforts on our behalf.

Certainly, we should not overwork our thank-you approach. I am not suggesting a constant stream of paper gratuities. Used sensibly, however, an expression of genuine appreciation can work wonders in future motivation.

Suppose you send me information I need. I respond, saying "thank you" and, perhaps, how I used your information. How are you going to feel on subsequent occasions when I come to you looking for additional assistance? I recognized your individual effort before and you probably will feel less put-upon in satisfying my current request.

You may be thinking a thank-you can be done even more informally on the telephone. I agree. A telephone call is especially effective when we must express appreciation frequently and writing each time would be too much of a good thing. I do like to see some thank-yous in writing, however, with a copy forwarded to the reader's boss. Complaints always move up one level, don't they? Yet you know as well as I do, we hesitate to go to our boss to repeat a complimentary telephone call or suggest he or she read a memo praising our performance.

Congratulations on personal achievement can also be extended to those readers we deal with on a continuing basis. I often send a letter or memo to someone saying something like "Congratulations, Joe, on your promotion." Certainly, the pat on the back is deserved. I also have improved the working relationship between Joe and myself through recognition of Joe's success. I could just as easily write, "Congratulations, Joe, on your election to the school board," or mention any other community-oriented accomplishment. Again, I'm building a communication bridge between myself and my reader.

Good judgment is also required in acknowledging personal achievement. I would *not* say, "Congratulations, Joe, on your new daughter," in a piece of Systems Documentation. That's totally inappropriate. If I were sending individual copies of a memo to a distribution list including Joe, however, I could hand-write at the bottom of his copy, "Congratulations on your new daughter." Joe will feel good about my recognition of an event important to him. I feel good in extending such recognition. We've put our business relationship into a human context.

Modern corporations and institutions become larger and more bureaucratic each year. What could be more vital to productive interaction in such organizations than the widespread patterns of cooperation fostered by personalized communication?

3. Relate to your reader's needs, his problems, his importance to your success.

Most of us try to relate to reader need—we have to meet it. We also identify with our reader's problems—we usually have to solve them. What concerns me is our unwillingness in data processing to acknowledge the reader's crucial role in *our* success.

It does not matter how experienced we are, how great our creativity and expertise. If the reader does not accept and utilize what we offer, we fail. Being brilliant technically may bring personal satisfaction, but reader acceptance sets the standard for professional accomplishment. How's your batting average?

Too many of our innovative ideas are being lost. Every day, I see constructive suggestions to improve and facilitate data processing applications die unheroically in someone's file drawer. We all know the ideas themselves are good. What is happening during their presentation to turn the user (and ultimate benefactor) into an adamant opponent of progress?

I think I have at least part of the answer. All of us are paid problem solvers. Whatever our area of data processing specialization, we spend the bulk of our time solving problems, often under the additional pressure of a crisis atmosphere. Naturally, the problems before us quickly become *our* problems, one more burden in an already overcrowded day. We have stopped asking the crucial question, "Whose problem is it?"

Perhaps we should start asking.

Yes, we have responsibility for solving the problem, but we are not locked into it. Our reader is.

Yes, we have to put the pieces together, but we don't have to live with the end result. Our reader does.

The problem is the reader's, and he knows it. People are almost as possessive of their problems as they are of their names.

Let's take a typical situation.

I come to you with a problem. If I could solve it myself, I wouldn't need you. Already, I feel at a disadvantage. I'm dependent on your expertise and professional judgment. Of course, I hope you'll do the best you can for me. Prior experience, however, tells me I'm in over my head with such things as technical considerations and jargon. I also don't see how my problem can ever be as important to you as it is to me. My attitude has to be ambivalent, wavering between high expectations and knowing I'm going to be stalled or downright conned.

Meanwhile, back at the department, you do your homework and come up with an excellent solution. You write it up and present it to me, with all the bells and whistles.

Unfortunately, I'm not sure. I wasn't involved in the behind-the-scenes effort and fail to fully understand your reasoning. I'm probably going to reject your excellent solution, not with specific objections but with the familiar, "You didn't understand"—"My people can't live with that"—"This is not what we wanted." Now, the communication channel is hopelessly fogged by frustration and resentment on both sides.

Back up. You know the problem is mine. Why not acknowledge that fact from the beginning? Voluntarily include me in the problem-solving process by encouraging my participation. You might say: "Rändi, you've been living with this situation. Could you help us by pointing out any direction we should explore, any area you see as important?"

Bingo. By inviting me in, you're already 80% of the way home. I now know you recognize the problem as mine and you're taking my involvement seriously.

I probably can't come up with much. Again, if I could, I wouldn't need you. But I just might come up with something—"It always happens when we use form XYZ"—"The information is wrong at the end of the quarter." Isn't this the type of trivia that inevitably surfaces too late? Readers consistently wait until you outline your solution to announce, "In Massachusetts, you can't do that." Involve me directly and you not only foster reader commitment, you make your own job easier. You gain access to information you need when it is most easily used—at the initiation of a project or service.

Once you elicit my contribution, you proceed as before. You do your homework and come up with an excellent solution. Now, however, when you present it, you are able to incorporate my small suggestions with appropriate credit. How will I view your ideas this time? I'm going to like them. You've made me an advocate of your solution in my department or organization. At the least, I will try it before complaining about it, great progress in some corporations. You sold me with the simple psychological principle of ownership. Your solution is now partially mine, and believe me, anything that is mine has got to be good.

Do notice this. The overall solution in both approaches will probably be exactly the same. All that makes the difference between acceptance and rejection is sensible communication.

E. Eliminate cliches, safe thoughts, and worn-out phrases.

Cliches make any written material appear "old hat." They make creative suggestions sound like "tried and true" formulas. Eliminate them.

I am particularly opposed to the homily approach where a Management Report is introduced with an "appropriate" quotation that is usually totally inappropriate. One I've seen 15 times in the past year is "Honest men pay their debts," a self-evident statement applicable to nothing.

The only way cliches work in business writing is when they are twisted to lend humor. I have no objection to humor in business. In fact, some situations cry out for it. I do, however, have two severe cautions if you plan to be a comedian.

After paraphrasing, humor is the most difficult form of writing. Unless you are adept at it, don't try it. The transition from verbal remark to typed joke is never easy.

For example, in a verbal context, I could drop my head to my desk, yawn vehemently, and listlessly remark, "This book is really terrific." You'd know I was being facetious. My tone of voice, facial expression, and entire body English would tell you so. Type that same statement out in black and white and it is etched in stone—with only one interpretation, the wrong one, possible.

Humor requires knowing not only your reader, but any possible audience, extremely well. Say you and I work together. I'm your liaison from a user area. We are well acquainted, and both of us find the same things screamingly funny. I can write a memo that makes my day. You get it, and the "funnies" make your day. Unfortunately, however, that memo contains information you must pass on to your boss. What are the odds he or she will find the same things funny that you and I do? In my experience, a flat zero.

Safe thoughts or say-nothing abstractions, as I call them, appear most frequently when business writers present concept. The best example is the stereotyped use of PURPOSE, DEFINITION, and SCOPE as headings in a Management Report.

SCOPE is a mouthwash. I have yet to see anyone write anything definitive under that heading. Most people reading Management Reports flip over such sections entirely looking for the good stuff. They've learned, as I have, that SCOPE is generally a paraphrase of DEFINITION, and DEFINITION, of course, is a paraphrase of PURPOSE.

Some of you may be locked into these headings by corporate standards or policy. Unfortunately, I am not in a position to start a palace revolt in your organization. Just know enough not to waste much time constructing these segments of your report. You may be the only one to read them.

Where possible, make headings pertinent to material covered in subsequent paragraphs. Introduce basic subject matter—higher salaries, new data processing system, defined parameters of a study—in concrete terms. Approach all content as important to the reader, and offer a saleable product that attracts reader interest rather than repels it. Also, remember, readers much prefer to feel they have reached any universal or abstract conclusions on their own.

Overused words and worn-out phrases are language appearing so consistently in business documents, any semblance of impact or even definition is lost.

For example, new data processing systems (when proposed) are inevitably described as "time-saving," "labor-saving," and "money-saving." No one believes these unimaginative conventions any more, particularly since these attributes often disappear by implementation. Suppose by some miracle we did come up with a time-saving, labor-saving, and money-saving system. To get reader attention, we should present specific data showing how much time, how many people, how much money—preferably in some sort of contrast with the manual or automated approach the user has currently. Now we're hitting readers where they live. They still may not agree, but at least we've established enough credibility that they'll read carefully—the first step in the sales process.

Another example. Most job applicants in organizations I visit are described at one time or another as "well-educated." The few who aren't are invariably "poised."

"Well-educated"—how?—for what purpose? Is this individual a skilled, autonomous problem solver, or am I going to have to hold his hand until he gets oriented? These are the reader's questions.

"Poised." That's like saying a girl is "nice." You know, "She's a nice girl; she's got a great personality." We know immediately she's a dog. If the individual describing her had *anything* to say, he'd say it. It's the same with "poised." That word can mean anything from sophisticated to good dresser, and usually winds up meaning the writer didn't know what else to say.

How about new procedures, administrative or technical? In data processing, we consistently describe new methods of doing anything as "dynamic" and "far-reaching." That is, of course, if they are not "somewhat unique."

What readers would like is some idea of the impact of the change on their job responsibilities, their departments or organizations. What they don't like are glowing but nonspecific hymns of praise.

F. Watch out for "Red Flag" words.

"Red Flag" words automatically evoke a negative reaction from most readers. They easily create an unpleasant tone. They also are often misinterpreted, particularly in a complaint situation.

Here are some examples to avoid:

"Frankly, this is your responsibility . . . ."

Whenever I see "frankly," I suspect (and so do most readers) that the writer is not being frank. If he were, he would not be so careful to assure me of his honesty. In data processing recently, I've seen increasing use of the more sophisticated "candidly." Reader reaction is exactly the same.

"You *claim* we did (not) . . . ."

This simply calls your reader a liar. His response is a defensive and often angry, "I don't *claim* anything. I know you did (not) . . . ."

"I know exactly how *you feel* . . . ."
"*You feel* . . . ."

Have you ever been badly frustrated by a problem, only to have the person creating the difficulty in the first place say condescendingly, "I know exactly how you feel"? What is your reaction? Mine has always been, "You don't know how I feel, but I'd be happy to tell you"—in triplicate and up at least one level. Subjective pronouncements are never acceptable in business. The patronizing tone suggested here can only exacerbate an already uncomfortable situation. You *don't* know how or what your reader "feels."

"This was *unavoidable* . . . ."

If we tell our reader a problem was "unavoidable," what are we telling him must reoccur a week, six months, or a year from now? What have we also just told him about our ability to meet his needs?

"This was an *inadvertent* error . . . ."

All the rest of your mistakes were planned.

"*If* we made an error . . . ."

Readers interpret this as a classic pass-the-buck routine. It suggests the reader is either stupid or lying. Even worse, how can a writer who refuses to admit an error has even been made, correct it?

"On the *contrary* . . . ."
"*Contrary* to your letter . . . ."

The tone here is argumentative. Such an approach immediately puts any reader on the defensive about his original position. What will now commence is a debate, not a dialogue.

"This is our *standard* approach . . . ."

If anyone brings a problem to you, the last thing he or she wants is "standard operating procedure." Everyone wants, some demand, personal and individualized attention. Even if you are going to handle a request or problem with SOP, don't be foolish enough to tip off your reader.

"*Past history* indicates . . . ."

All this tells me is that I'm going to get the same lousy service from you now and in the future that I've received in the past.

"I'm sorry, but we must go with requests of higher *priority* . . . ."

"Priority" is the established data processing cop-out. We use it as an excuse for the majority of our negative judgments. Priority is determined by job-related factors—fixed schedules, budgetary restrictions, personnel allocation. These specifics are certain to be more acceptable to any reader than an implication that his request is not as important as someone else's. The only way a reader likes this overworked word is when we write, "You are our number one priority".

I've mentioned only a few of the "Red Flag" words prevalent in business writing. The best way to identify the other nonproductive words circulating in your organization is to check your in-box. What words in your reading set you off? A negative or argumentative response on your part is an excellent clue to the probable reaction of your reader.

It's simple. Don't unto others . . . .

7
Key V—
Plain Speech

This is perhaps the most difficult Key. It requires discarding traditional business presentation and learning to write in a natural, straightforward style.

A. Be confident.

This may sound like a deodorant commercial, but it's important. Good writing requires self-confidence. It demands not only confidence in our writing ability, but confidence in our knowledge of our material. The less we know about a subject, the more we write in confusing generalities. We either don't know the specifics or we are reluctant to include the few we do know for fear of sparking questions.

Many of us do write about unfamiliar topics. We do so because of increasing management pressure to come up with instantaneous solutions. For one reason or another, if we are unable to respond immediately when a problem is presented to us, our credibility is somehow called into question. I'm sure you've seen people give in to this competitive urgency and shoot from the hip, figuring anything is better than nothing. Data processors are famous for "faking" it.

Unfortunately, sooner or later, we have to go in with specifics. Now, however, we're usually dealing with a reader who has made up his mind. One who has reached certain conclusions based on insufficient or even inaccurate information. We may actually have to change his viewpoint. Writing convincingly is difficult enough. Writing when we are not sure of what we're doing can make it impossible.

Why not be willing to honestly explain the situation to your reader? When necessary, spell out the time framework required. Give your reader a date on which he can expect a complete response. You might write something like: "I will need approximately two weeks to do the work necessary to answer your questions adequately. You will have an answer no later than January 16."

This buys you time. Time to investigate and then make realistic analytical or administrative decisions. Readers generally accept such delays because they know they will hear from you by a specific date. They also see the improved quality of the end result. On your side of the fence, the entire task is more manageable because you are out from under the gun.

Know enough to be confident with your subject matter and to be sure of your objective in writing. Remember, confidence is contagious. Try to provide fully for your reader's needs with one well-written and comprehensive document. Less work for you. More satisfaction for your reader.

Here's my rule of thumb. If you aren't ready to write, *don't*.

B. Use contemporary expressions.

I am not suggesting any special effort to be "hip" or use words out of cigarette commercials. I am suggesting, however, that you write as closely as possible to the way in which you speak. The written word is never exactly the same as the spoken word, but using patterns of speech natural to your conversation makes your writing an accurate reflection of you as an individual.

It also increases reader comprehension. Have you ever received a written explanation of something and simply not understood it? You call the writer, ask for clarification, and what miraculously occurs the minute he begins to *talk* about his subject? You understand it, don't you? If that writer had written his material in the way he verbalizes it, your telephone call would have been totally unnecessary.

I don't know the amount of profanity in your personal vocabulary, but with that exception, colloquial expressions, some slang, even street language, lend clarity and emphasis to what you write. They are perfectly acceptable in most business communities when used within reasonable limitations. Certainly, they make any written material more interesting to read.

Changing Times Magazine provided a thought-provoking example. One article quoted Micawber, from the book *David Copperfield*. Someone makes the mistake of asking Micawber what he does for a living. He replies:

"I am at present engaged in the sale of corn on commission. It is not an avocation of remunerative description."

Picture yourself at a cocktail party. You ask some guy what he does, and he lays that on you. How would you react? I'd have to get another drink. What Micawber is saying, of course, is:

"I sell corn on commission. The pay's lousy."

We often write using language we hope will make us appear knowledgeable and erudite (see, I know the big words also). Unfortunately, in all too many instances, we wind up sounding as pompous and ridiculous as Micawber. Have you ever received a memorandum or letter, read it, and thought to yourself, "Who does this guy think he is?" We certainly do not want our readers to form any such impression of us.

The use of pretentious words and phrasing is incredibly widespread in business writing. Take this closing sentence from a memo I reviewed:

"Please endeavor to continue to perform the above mentioned functions in the prescribed manner."

Sounds obscene, doesn't it? I was delighted—finally an X-rated memorandum. To my distress, however, I had missed the above mentioned functions altogether, so I reread the document. What do you suppose the writer was actually talking about? He was using praise as a motivational technique, standard management theory. What he meant was:

"You're doing a great job. Keep it up."

Which would more highly motivate you—the first version or the second? Unhappily, which sounds more familiar in most business environments?

C. Explain your jargon.

We can't discuss PLAIN SPEECH without getting into the question of jargon. Jargon, of course, is defined as specialized terminology or buzz words. Every professional group in the United States has some—lawyers, doctors, insurance salespeople. The difficulty has been that data processors have more than anyone else, and we *use* ours more than any other profession uses its jargon. I'm convinced we employ jargon as much as we do for two simple reasons:

I just suggested we should use patterns of speech natural to our conversation in our writing. Jargon is natural for us. We use it daily among ourselves and easily forget that individuals outside our frame of reference (or even in a different data processing specialty) may not understand or may define terms differently.

Jargon is a great way to preserve the old data processing mystique. Whenever we want to, we can shut out just about any other individual or group. Our fog index is unbelievably high. We even out-mystique each other. All you have to do to catch this act is to be at a party when two people find out they both are in data processing. What follows is the "war of the words," all to prove "My technical background and my systems are certainly more sophisticated than yours, fella."

Unfortunately, our use of jargon, for whatever reason, has built a language barrier between us and user or management areas even within our own organizations. People do not ask questions. Why? Consider this. Computer technology is a fact of everyone's life, professional and personal. For anyone in contemporary business to admit he doesn't understand data processing terminology is for him to announce he hasn't kept up with the times. No one willingly admits such ignorance. In my experience, readers react to unfamiliar words or phrases in one of two ways:

They ignore the word altogether, meaning you will never be on the same wavelength.

They make up their own definition and they share it with others. Now, you're not dealing with one dummy, you're dealing with a department full of dummies, few of whom will ever acknowledge their error.

Many data processors have said to me: "Rändi, *everyone* understands data processing jargon. It's just not a problem." I heard this often enough that I felt I had better test comprehension levels, just to be sure.

In one seminar I conducted, half the participants were data processors, half users. I asked the users to bring in any memorandums or letters they had received containing data processing buzz words. The first one presented had a dynamite opening sentence. It said:

"Your system crashed."

Now, where you go from there with a user, I'm not sure. "OK," I said to the user, "your system crashed. What do you think that means?" His response: "Well, Rändi, I'm not sure. I guess it means the whole thing sort of *fell over* . . . . " You notice he didn't ask.

Another classic example came in the last sentence of a brief proposal. It read:

"Your system will require a dedicated on-line printer."

Everyone knows about "dedicated" and on-line printers, but I did ask the user his interpretation. "Can you believe it?" he exclaimed angrily. "They've got all those printers down in operations. Now they want my department to buy one and they're going to put a plaque on it saying DEDICATED BY . . . . "

I think my point is made.

Where you can, avoid jargon entirely. Where you can't, be willing to explain it:

"Your system will require a dedicated (for your use only) on-line printer."

I would much prefer to see you err in the direction of too much explanation rather than too little. If you have many necessary jargon terms, don't define each in the context of your document, but do enclose a glossary. The glossary approach allows each reader to determine whether he or she should check the definition of a word or phrase. This is particularly valuable when you have multiple readers, some who may need assistance, others who would be bored by constant explanation. You'll also find that even readers who ordinarily would assume they understood your jargon will check their interpretation if a glossary is available.

Be particularly careful with acronyms. We use them consistently to refer to systems, software, areas of responsibility, everything. Spell them out for your reader, at least the first time. Most acronyms don't mean much even where we know the words they represent, but at least you and your reader should start at the same level of confusion.

One additional caution with acronyms. Try to develop sensible ones. Too many are jokes, some not acceptable to any user. Even in many data processing groups, the proliferation of acronyms has become a recognized farce. Take a look below at this delightful acronym commentary from the Aetna Variable Annuity Life Insurance Company in Hartford, Connecticut.

Aetna Variable Annuity Life Insurance Company

INTER-OFFICE COMMUNICATION

TO Dean E. Wolcott, Senior Vice President
FROM Kenneth P. Veit, Vice President, Operations
DATE June 10, 1975
SUBJECT ACRONYMS AT AVAR

For your handy reference, the following is a list of all major acronyms currently being used by AVAR. We currently have a pending Class 34 position open for a Manager of Acronym Development (MAD). He will be known as the MAD-man (unless female). Some have suggested that I be considered for the position.

ADVANCE	Inforce data base
CENSURE	Single broker-dealer project committee
CONGA	Pension case administration system
CRUNCH	Deregistration project committee
DEIFIC	Data element ident for integrated construction
DYSMAL*	Systems Dynamics project
IMPACT	New paid production system
IMPEL	New persistency system
INCOMM	New commission system project
PLUMMET	Project team which is defining IMPEL
PRAVDA	New product project
PROMISE	D.P. project control system
SCRAPE**	Pension administration project committee
SMERSH	PRAVDA control group
TACTICS	General ledger accounting system
VARSEC	D.P. Steering Committee

*A new one: *DY*namic *S*ystem *M*odel of *A*ll *L*osses
**Another new one: *S*elect *C*ommittee to *R*eorganize *A*dministration of *P*ensions *E*ffectively

·Mr. Veit later wrote to tell me, ". . . in the interest of terminological exactitude you should be aware that the acronym DYSMAL was subsequently changed to AVALANCHE which stands for *A*etna *V*ariable *A*nalyzer of *L*osses *A*ctuaries *N*ever *C*ould *H*ope to *E*xplain."

As a personal sidelight, the only acronym I've ever seen employed completely without question was a system called GARBAGE. I always had a feeling the user didn't ask what it meant because he knew.

I also suggest referencing hardware by purpose, not model number. I once saw a memorandum with fourteen model numbers in three paragraphs. It looked like a Sears catalog run amok. You can always include model numbers if they're important, but remember, users identify hardware by its function, what it does.

Certainly, our concern with definition of jargon must be tempered by the sophistication of our various users. Some require more explanation than others. Also, in defining our terms for a user, we are performing an educational function, hopefully cutting down on the amount of clarification needed on subsequent occasions.

Increasingly, in visiting data processing shops across the country, I find a new wrinkle in our jargon usage. Not content with our own computer terminology, we have added so-called management jargon to our repertoire. Management jargon, of course, is the combination of at least three obfuscating words to replace a single, simple one.

Let me demonstrate. Below is a BAFFLE-GAB THESAURUS. It is *not* an educational aid. I offer it only to show you how common a problem management jargon actually is in business writing.

BAFFLE-GAB THESAURUS*

0)	Integrated	Management	Options
1)	Total	Organizational	Flexibility
2)	Systematized	Monitored	Capability
3)	Parallel	Reciprocal	Mobility
4)	Functional	Digital	Programming
5)	Responsive	Logistical	Concept
6)	Optional	Transitional	Time-Phase
7)	Synchronized	Incremental	Projection
8)	Compatible	Third-generation	Hardware
9)	Balanced	Policy	Contingency

*Originally developed in the Royal Canadian Air Force, the *BAFFLE-GAB THESAURUS* was popularized by Philip Broughton, a U.S. Public Health Service official.

As you see, the BGT is set up so anyone can choose any three digit number, select the corresponding buzz words from the three columns and come up with a phrase that rings with authority and means absolutely nothing.

The use of these phrases seems to occur in cycles. I will see one for awhile, then its popularity wanes and another replaces it. For example, the current favorite is right off the top—Integrated Management Options. Since "integrated" and "optional" are somewhat opposed in meaning, no one defines that in exactly the same way as anyone else. The most widely used phrase over the last five years is number 1—Total Organizational Flexibility—translated *chaos*.

I would like you to note number 8—Compatible Third-generation Hardware. Most of us could define that, at least to our own satisfaction. This is not a list of data processing jargon, however. It's a list of management or user buzz words. Every piece of hardware I've recently seen referenced in a user document has been described as "compatible"—translated *friendly*.

Please don't rip the BGT out of the book, laminate it, and tape it to your desk for easy reference. Too much of this nonsense is already in circulation. Recognize how this use of language bogs down all business communication and let it stop with you.

D. Be aware of sentence construction.

Let's spend a few minutes on straight writing technique.

The average reader can absorb just so much physically in terms of concentration and mentally in terms of comprehension, and then he takes a break. Physically, he blinks—no one can stare indefinitely at typed words. Mentally, he shifts gears, stopping thought interpretation. The average absorption rate nationwide is *20* words. That's it. Some studies place the figure at 24, but I find 20 a better average.

This means our optimum sentence length is 20 words. Now, I'm not suggesting you actually count the words in your sentences. That's too time-consuming and probably nonproductive anyway, particularly since you know when you've gone considerably over 20 words. You've used a phrase like "provided that" or "in case of" or employed a conjunction like "and"—"and"—"and." Just remember, if you go considerably over 20 words, you've made it *physically* impossible for your reader to understand you. It doesn't matter how highly motivated he may be. The best rule of thumb is to strive for *one* thought in *one* sentence.

Of course, all sentences of exactly 20 words would be incredibly boring to read. The best approach is to intersperse longer sentences with shorter sentences, each serving a different function.

Longer sentences—up to and including, but rarely more than, 28 words— physically retard the reader on the page. They slow him down. Shorter sentences are more abrupt and staccato. They speed the reader down the page, making excellent transitional sentences. If you are having difficulty with transition points and your content is correct, check sentence length. You probably are ending one thought with a long sentence and beginning the next with a long sentence. Again, this makes it physically impossible for your reader to make the mental jump.

If the average comprehension rate is 20 words, obviously the first 20 words you write are the most important. Many readers make a mental judgment whether or not to take a document seriously based on the opening 20 words. Maybe you do this yourself. How many times do you know instantly, "This is important"? And how often do you decide, "Here we go again. I only need to skim this one"? Yet, we consistently throw away this crucial introduction with hackneyed phrases like, "This is in reference to your memo of June 19 regarding . . . ." The reader tunes out.

Here are some ways to make your first sentence a "Grabber"—have it reach out, attract, and hold reader interest:

1. Make your first sentence your first paragraph. Surrounding a thought with white space lends physical emphasis and creates a pause for greater comprehension.

2. Ask a rhetorical question. Yes, you're going to proceed to answer it, but we're all conditioned to respond to a question mark. Your reader instinctively answers your question mentally. He is involved with your subject matter whether he wants to be or not.

3. Make a controversial statement. Readers who agree will willingly read on to have their own opinion substantiated. Those who disagree read carefully in order to marshal ammunition for an argument.

4. Concisely state your objective. If you've defined it carefully, putting what is most important to your reader first, he's hooked.

Experiment with your own formulas for a first sentence, 20-word "Grabber." Currently, close to 60% of the business documents I review are skimmed or not fully completed by their readers. Whether your letters and memos are among the remaining 40% that are carefully read is highly dependent on your sentence construction and placement. One thing for sure, we have to get read to have even a chance at meeting our objectives.

E. Make paragraphs flow logically.

Paragraphs work much the same as sentences. Generally, they follow our predetermined sequence criteria (see "D" under The Think-Through, page 21.)

Be careful with this, however. If your first subject area is extensive, you could wind up in the unfortunate position of having your first paragraph be your first page. We all know our reaction to this unpleasant visual presentation. The document looks bulky and tedious, so no matter what the subject matter, it goes on the bottom of our "to be read" pile.

Again, we must vary our paragraph length. As with sentences, the best format is a mixture of sizes for variety and smooth transition. If your first sentence is not your first paragraph, then your entire opening paragraph should be developed as a "Grabber."

Perhaps the most crucial element to data processors in paragraph construction is the placement of "interruptions." An interruption occurs whenever you distract reader attention from your primary or cover document, directing him to an exhibit. This happens most frequently and is most important in Management Reports and interpretative formats such as the Proposal or Feasibility Study.

Let's begin by considering the *Business Appendix*. Not an Academic Appendix, now, but the accepted business application. Anytime you present more than three exhibits of any kind—charts, tables, graphs, illustrations, or enclosed copies— you have a Business Appendix. A Business Appendix, by definition, must carry its own Table of Contents. I think you can see how necessary this is, particularly in our industry. More often than not, our exhibits are used as a separate reference entity, apart from our cover document. Certainly, we don't want our readers to have to continually flip through a lengthy report or memorandum to identify and utilize our exhibits properly.

Suppose you prepare a Feasibility Study with six associated exhibits. Further, suppose I, your reader, must examine Exhibit 6 *prior* to reading the explanation of Exhibit 6 in your cover report. If I don't review the exhibit first, I won't understand your explanation. Where then must the interruption or the sentence, "See Exhibit 6," go on the page?

Most writers make the interruption the first sentence in their paragraph of explanation. They write, "See Exhibit 6," and continue their remarks. Unfortunately, the natural human tendency is to keep reading the remainder of the paragraph. Readers do this and are thoroughly confused when they finally do refer to Exhibit 6—usually after completing the entire paragraph.

"See Exhibit 6" should be a separate, single sentence paragraph directly preceeding your paragraph of explanation. The reader reads it, is stopped by the white space, and turns compliantly to Exhibit 6. He reviews the exhibit and returns to your cover document, finding his place easily, as the interruption paragraph stands out on the page. He will begin reading where he should—at your paragraph of explanation—relating it directly to the exhibit he just reviewed.

Suppose, however, your reader must read your explanation of Exhibit 6 *prior* to looking at the exhibit itself or the exhibit will make no sense. Now, where would you place the interruption, "See Exhibit 6," on the page? It should, of course, go at the end of your explanation. This time, however, it is not broken out as a separate paragraph. You want your reader to connect what he just read with the exhibit he will see. Consequently, the interruption should be the final sentence in your paragraph of explanation, set out in parenthesis:

"(See Exhibit 6.)"

Your reader goes immediately to the exhibit, reviewing it in the context of your explanation. When he returns to your cover document, he easily locates his place through the visual reference of the parenthesis. He again begins reading where he should, maintaining orderly transition from point to point.

Interruptions are never used in the middle of a paragraph. Such placement breaks a reader's train of thought at an awkward moment. Again, most readers will finish the entire paragraph before referencing the exhibit. In addition, they now must reread at least part of the cover document to find the buried interruption sentence and their place in your content. Continuity between explanation and exhibit is lost.

With most of the data processing exhibits I review, the material is excellent. I do find, however, that many interruptions are reversed in their usage or carelessly positioned. Place your interruptions to ensure your illustrations and exhibits are a visual *aid,* not a hindrance to reader comprehension.

8
Key VI—
Salesmanship

People do make judgments based on what they see on paper. Whatever you write in a business context reflects directly on you, your group or department, and—if you communicate with outside vendors or clients—your corporation.

Using this Key, you can write to sell your personal creativity and expertise, the competency of your area as a whole, the good name of your entire organization. These techniques help you show who you are and what you are capable of providing. They create a service-oriented and individualized tone in any business document, from the highly structured to the more informal.

A. Use names.

Show your reader you recognize the importance of individual responsibility. Use the proper name of anyone directly involved with your subject. Traditional business writing, unfortunately, has encouraged the use of words that do not adequately represent people. For instance, I consistently see sentences like the following:

"The aforementioned was in this office in November."

We all use the *aforementioned,* the *above,* the *below,* the *preceding.* Often there are so many of these anonymous references, readers cannot determine which person or persons the writer is discussing. I even saw one memorandum stating:

"This was referred to a *certain party* in the Marketing Department."

That sounds almost illicit. The tone is certainly one of indecisive buck-passing. Why not simply personalize both sentences?

"Mr. Michaels was here in November."
"I referred this to Ms. James in Marketing."

We, of course, would not want to keep repeating "Mr. Michaels," or any other name, throughout our document. What could we substitute for name, without resorting to impersonal designation?

One suggestion would be personal pronouns. Once we introduce "Mr. Michaels," we certainly can use "he" in subsequent references. We could say "John Michaels" and use "John" where first name is appropriate. If we identify John's position, we can use his title—giving personal recognition to John and conveying valuable information to our reader at the same time.

I also like to see words like "associate" or "colleague." Most other professional groups use these to good advantage. Data processors, so far, have not. By definition, these terms create a sense of expertise. They suggest cooperative effort directed toward a common goal. Both are particularly appropriate if you employ the team concept in your organization and more than one individual has responsibility for a specific project or service.

"My associate and I will meet you Monday at 4 P.M."

One caution. Whenever you reference anyone in anything you write, he or she receives a copy. I'm sure you would expect similar courtesy from anyone who cited you in his letter or memorandum. Here's another good reason. None of us in business likes surprises. Yet, how often has someone linked you to something you didn't find out about until questions or problems developed? The use of so-called blind copies prevents free and often necessary circulation of material. Even worse, they can cause those involved to eventually appear disorganized or deliberately secretive.

The same rule applies when your comment is negative. Always copy all individuals whose names you use. In many organizations, unpleasant news reaches these people anyway via the grapevine—usually exaggerated and out-of-context. Certainly, it's better for all concerned if any negative remarks come directly from you. Misunderstanding is avoided. Any possible disagreements are open to discussion.

B. Don't be afraid of personal pronouns.

Personal pronouns became standard business practice about ten years ago. For data processors, once locked into stylized technical formats, they've developed into an excellent and easily used personalization device.

They are, however, often abused. The most persistent difficulty with pronoun usage has been the opportunity they present any writer who wants to cop-out on responsibility. For instance, have you ever tried to determine who *we* represents?

"We decided on this approach."

Who's *we*? Is it a department, the company itself, a group of friends at lunch? I always have a vision of everyone in an organization getting together to take a vote. How about *they*?

"They say your request is not feasible."

This pronoun is particularly offensive when used editorially, as it most often appears in negative statements. Have you ever attempted to pin down the "they" in every organization who decide something cannot or will not be done? Who are *they*? The tone created is of an irrevocable brick wall—almost "God speaks." The inevitable reader reaction is frustration and resistance.

Ask yourself, "For whom am I speaking?" prior to writing any document. If you are representing departmental action or decision-making, be sure your reader knows this.

"The Data Processing Department reviews all development requests as received. *We* have placed your XYZ system on the agenda of *our* next interdepartmental meeting."

If you are presenting corporate or organization policy, spell it out.

"Data Operations, Inc. no longer solicits transformation contracts. However, *we'll* be delighted to review your other data processing needs."

If you did it—if you made the decision, provided the information, whatever— the proper pronoun, of course, is I.

"I've logged your scheduling request for August. Anything new for September, please call *me* at ext. 374."

At one time in business communication, the pronoun *I* was never used. This has not been true for at least five years. None of us wants to write an ego-tripping document with each sentence beginning *I, I, I*. This shuts off any reader. Most readers, however, are grateful for writers who are willing to assume at least some individual and easily recognized responsibility.

Mark Twain once said, "No one has the right to use the editorial *we* or the editorial *they* unless he is

1. a monarch
2. a newspaper publisher
3. an individual with a tape worm."

It's a good rule of thumb to keep in mind.

Let's review the use of personal pronouns historically to see exactly what we've accomplished. Prior to the acceptance of personal pronouns, we would have said:

"It has been determined by the Accounting Department that . . . ."

Such a statement is automatically passive and wordy. It also forces a nonproductive "that" phrase.

Then personal pronouns were introduced and the sentence became more conversational:

"Our Accounting Department tells me . . . ."

That's not bad. Tone is certainly improved. Fewer words are required. There is still a problem, however. Suppose you direct that statement to me, proceeding to outline data furnished by the Accounting Department and how you'll use it to test my new system. Further, suppose I think that data stinks. I feel it's invalid and definitely will not produce a representative test of system capability.

Who am I going to contact?

I've been around organizations a long time. I know better than to shoot blind into the Accounting Department. I do have a name and a number, however—yours. I'm coming directly to you with my complaint.

You, unfortunately, can't handle it. All you can say to me is: "Rändi, I didn't come up with that data. You'll have to contact so-and-so (and he *is* a so-and-so) in the Accounting Department."

I now call the guy in Accounting. He says: "Rändi, I was on vacation. You'll have to talk to———." I call———and she says, "Rändi, I had yellow jaundice that week, you'll have to talk to ———."

By the time I reach the poor individual who did develop that data—after being bumped telephone extension to telephone extension—am I still calm and rational? I doubt it. I'm now convinced you, your department, and the Accounting Department are joined in a conspiracy of incompetence.

What about the performance level of the person who must ultimately deal with me? He will probably be incapable of adequately defending either his original data or his department's efficiency. He's *not* prepared for my telephone call. I'm coming right off the wall at him—an uncomfortable, and possibly disastrous, surprise.

Let's back up. What could you add to "Our Accounting Department tells me . . . ." that would avoid such a vicious communication circle altogether?

How about a specific name?

"Bob Buehrer in the Accounting Department tells me . . . ."

Now if I question the data you're using, I'm going *directly* to Bob Buehrer. I should be easier to deal with, even in a complaint atmosphere, because I only had to make *one* call. There's no buildup of anger or frustration. Also, Bob now has a chance to explain his viewpoint and back up his department's actions. Neither my telephone call, nor my subject matter should catch him unprepared. Remember, you mentioned him by name in your original document. Therefore, he received a copy.

This is the way business communication is supposed to work.

C. Little things mean a lot.

Here are three small details in business writing that affect writer success far out of proportion to their overall significance. The misuse of any one of them can completely negate an otherwise well-written document.

1. Spelling and punctuation

My name is R-ä-n-d-i with an umlaut over the a. It's Norwegian in origin and pronounced Ron-die. I'm the eighth generation Rändi in my family. My daughter is the ninth. We have no originality whatsoever. It is, however, *my* name and anytime I receive something addressed to *Rhondie* or *Randy,* I am predisposed to ignore the contents. After all, the writer has not afforded me the simple courtesy of spelling my name correctly. I do not expect the umlaut (although I often get it), but I do expect *Randi*. Last year, I actually received a letter beginning:

"Thank you *Bonnie* . . . ."

What possible effect could such a thank-you have? I react negatively when addressed incorrectly, and I think you'll find other readers are equally sensitive.

Now, I recognize that my name is a difficult one. Many more familiar names, however, also vary widely in spelling:

"John—Jon"
"Allen—Alan"
"Helen—Hellen"
"Robin—Robyn"

None of these individuals—nor any of hundreds of others—want to see their names misspelled.

This is the best reason I can think of for proofreading everything you write. Only you know the proper spelling of your respondent's name. Proofreading, of course, is particularly important if you dictate. Dictate "Jon" and you will probably get "John." Dictate "Ron-die" and heaven knows what you'll get—certainly not "Rändi."

Don't stop with checking your reader's name. Check your own. One woman in a seminar I conducted was named Suzanne. If you know any Suzannes, I'm sure you know it's totally unacceptable to shorten their name to Susan. This particular Suzanne had been receiving correspondence from her liaison in a user area consistently addressed to Susan. She finally called him, explained she didn't want to make a big deal out of it, but her name was *Suzanne*. The liaison said it wasn't a problem. He would be delighted to use Suzanne in the future. He did add, however, that he was a bit puzzled. All the communication he had received from her had been from *Susan*. She checked. It was.

Proofread your entire document. I often find executive correspondence with misspelled words, mispunctuation, phrases out of sync. Any document that goes out over your signature is a reflection of you. I don't believe any of us wishes that reflection to be one of carelessness at best, ignorance at worst.

Show your reader you take pride in your written work by correcting any and *all* typographical errors. There is no hard and fast rule that documents containing typos must be retyped. In many organizations, this could create an unacceptable time lag. Keep a black ink pen at your desk and manually correct minor errors before signing. This tells your reader you consider both the ideas you are presenting and his impression of them to be important. Of course, when to mark corrections and when to retype must be determined by each writer's situation. Although manual corrections are now generally accepted, there are documents—communication directed to clients, upper management, etc.—which should be done over.

2. Form of address

Form of address involves the words *Mr., Ms., Mrs.,* and *Miss.* These are not crucial to effective communication, of course, but use of the wrong one is definitely annoying to any reader. Some organizations have solved the problem by eliminating form of address altogether. They simply write "Dear Robin Evans:" rather than hassle over correct sex identity and marital status. Most of us, however, are still confronted with picking the appropriate designation, and it's not always an easy decision.

If you don't know the sex of your respondent—and some names can be either male or female—use full name. Guessing is a bad gamble. When you know your respondent is male, there is only one choice—Mr. Where you know your reader is female, proper choice is more difficult. Women can be *Ms., Mrs.,* or *Miss.* I suggest simplifying your selection by utilizing what is now an accepted nationwide standard—*Ms.* Whatever your feelings on Woman's Liberation and other volatile issues associated with this term, it is the easiest and generally, the most correct.

Let's take me as an example.

I am not "Mrs. Rändi Sigmund Smith" even socially, according to Amy Vanderbilt's Rules of Etiquette, unless I am either widowed or divorced. I am neither one. I am "Mrs. Richard Peter Smith," yet few of you would know my husband's name. I don't use it in my job. This almost puts you in the position of having to call me to ask, "Are you married?—widowed?—divorced? What is your husband's name?" All of which is a ridiculous exercise. Furthermore, many professional women retain their maiden names even though married. You also would have to ask, "Whose name are you using?" It's much simpler to go with Ms.

Women do, however, still have a choice. Their selection of form of address is indicated by their signature line. For instance, if I sign my name:

"Rändi S. Smith"

I am automatically *Ms.* Smith. If I wish the married designation, I must sign:

"Rändi S. Smith (Mrs. Richard P.)"

I am now *Mrs.* Smith or *Mrs.* Richard Smith. I am still not, however, *Mrs.* Rändi Smith. If I am unmarried and dislike the Ms., I indicate my preference by signing:

"(Miss) Rändi S. Smith"

Form of address must also be consistent within any document. Use either all first names or none. For example, if you begin "Mr. Jones," "Mr. Jackson," you would not then write "Rändi Smith," but "Ms. Smith." The reverse is also true. It is not correct to write "Michael Jones," "Jack Johnson," "Ms. Smith." Here, my first name should also appear.

One form of address no longer used is the traditional "Gentlemen:" This, of course, was a standard opening when the writer had no specific name in the organization he was addressing. In today's world, if you employ this device, your document inevitably winds up on the desk of a militant female. Where you don't have name, skip the formal salutation completely (See "D. Acknowledge Your Reader" under Word Selection, page 46.)

An additional change in proper usage of form of address is the acceptance of a woman's last name without one. At one time, any woman referenced in written material had to be identified as Mrs. or Miss. Now, from newspaper to business correspondence, last name alone is sufficient for men and women alike:

"Jones and Smith will direct development."

3. Distribution lists.

A writer is allowed *four* names in the "TO:" section of a memorandum. More than four names, and the heading becomes "TO: DISTRIBUTION," with the respondents' names appearing in list format elsewhere in the document. Some distribution lists are typed at the end of the last page of a memo. Others are arranged on a "Buck Slip."

Please check distribution lists in your area. I consistently review such lists only to find they contain names of people no longer even employed by the corporation. It's sad, but true. Once on a distribution list, always on a distribution list.

Any standing list should be updated on a quarterly basis. This update is not a clerical function, by the way, and shouldn't be foisted on secretaries or typists. Only you—the person who uses the list and understands its function—can adequately determine current status or changes to a reader's need-to-know.

The best lists contain *ten* names or less. If any of your lists must be larger, at least break them up for updating purposes. Go A to M, then N to Z, rotating from one to the other each quarter. Otherwise, updating and re-evaluation become too time-consuming and are usually discontinued.

Distribution lists are always arranged alphabetically—A to Z. Banks and insurance companies especially, but other industries as well, are often hung up on arranging such lists in *descending* order of rank. This simply doesn't work. Titles rarely correspond from one area of an organization to another. "What's higher?" is a familiar question. If you get two or more individuals of equal rank, you're into alpha-arrangement within rank. It can take thirty minutes to write a document and two hours to figure the distribution list.

Go A to Z. If position is important—and it can be in some instances—place the appropriate title after each individual's name.

Some of you may be distributing your material hand to hand or desk to desk within your departments via Buck Slip. If you are, here are two cautions:

Should your list be longer than ten names, split it up A to M, N to Z—and send at least two copies. My name is Smith and in many shops, I could receive the notice of a departmental picnic two weeks after the event. Internal lists cannot effectively contain more than ten names. When they do, some individuals never receive information while it is still pertinent.

Whenever any document goes out to an internal list over your signature, your name is *last* on the list. Have a line typed directly after the name normally in the last position. Type your name below the line, preceding "file" or whatever final destination is standard in your area.

McCarthy
Sheehan
Wristofak

———————————

Smith
FILE

When you are sending two or more copies, follow the same procedure on each list. This will prevent your getting your memorandum back before its complete distribution.

The reason for putting the writer's name last is a good one. It's easy to think everyone has access to your information as soon as a document is on its way. Actually, however, you can't assume anyone knows anything until after your memorandum returns to your desk and you see who checked off his name and who didn't. If you are not doing this now, you may be surprised at the time it can take for something to circulate. In large departments, particularly during peak vacation periods in July and August, I've seen it take six weeks to two months for a simple memo to make the rounds.

D. Write to make friends.

Many people in various organizations have come to me to say: "Rändi, I know how to write. You could not red pencil a single thing I put on paper. The problem is not me—it's my thick-headed readers. I just don't get any cooperation".

This often-expressed viewpoint concerns me. You notice I carefully stress effective *written communication* rather than straight writing skills. I do so for a reason. The ability to write does not, in and of itself, ensure that anyone is able to communicate. Writing skill only helps simplify the process. Good communication also requires *commitment*—the willingness to recognize communication as a crucial element in any business activity and the determination to make it work. Most people can write. It is only those who understand the need to reach others with what they write who communicate effectively.

No one can hold a gun to your head and insist, "You will communicate." Communication is too subjective a skill. People can and do, however, evaluate your communication abilities based on end result. Where objectives are accomplished, communication has usually been successful. Where constant problems or bad attitudes are the order of the day, poor communication is generally the culprit.

I have learned that anytime you take pen to paper, you either build a bridge or you burn one. I also find, in most organizations, that a bridge once burned tends to stay destroyed. You only need to burn about four of these communication bridges and your personal effectiveness in any working environment can be gone forever.

Let's take an example that demonstrates both the limits of writing skill and the relationship of good communication to productivity. I once did some consulting work in one department of a large corporation. During my visit, the department manager failed to receive some expected personnel files. They evidently had been misrouted or lost. He sent a simple memorandum to adjacent areas in an attempt to locate his material. He assumed, as I would, that each of his respondents would know people only ask for things they (or their management) think they need.

Here is the first response he received:

"No, we don't have the files you mentioned.

Personnel reports are rarely forwarded to our area.
Your routing slip must be in error."

This is extremely well written. It's brief and to the point with good sentence construction. Role-play for a moment, however, as if you were the manager who needed those files. How would you react to this reply? I wouldn't think this writer had even looked. His entire tone suggests he received the inquiry, thought "That's a stupid question," and shot off his answer.

The mills of the gods grind slowly in a business context. I know this. Within the next ten months, however, who would you guess will be coming in to us (the manager) looking for something? Our friend, the author? He'll need information, perhaps a decision. Is it even printable what we'll feel like telling him he can do with his request? He is now going to get exactly the type of communication he deserves. Yet, unfortunately, he is also the one who inevitably comes to me with the "I can write . . . " tale of woe.

I find this a great illustration of the Peter Principle, where one rises to one's highest level of inefficiency and sits there. This writer just burned a bridge. Remember, he only needs to burn about three more and he might as well be on the street. Addding to the tragedy is the fact he will probably never know *why* his career was sandbagged.

Now consider this second reply:

"Sorry, John, but we don't have the files you need. I have asked our supervisors to check carefully and they saw no sign of them. Perhaps the production department can help you. They often are next in line after us on routing slips."

This is not well written. For instance, it's somewhat overstated. Also, the writer should not point out that he asked his supervisors to check "carefully," implying they usually are sloppy. Role-play again, however, as the manager. How different would your reaction be to this response compared to the first? I would feel he recognized my need and he did look. Also, when he could not provide the requested material, he told me (in a nice way) where to go.

I'm back to the mills of the gods again, but within the next ten months, who else will come to us (still the manager) looking for something? Isn't it our not particularly skilled writer? I would never suggest to you that we will automatically give him the information or decision he seeks. We may not be able to. Isn't it true though that we will at least hear him out? Even if his subsequent request requires additional effort on our part, won't we be likely to try to meet it?

He's built a bridge. He also is going to get exactly the kind of communication he deserves—communication that in this case should heighten his individual productivity.

I like these two examples. Examining them and their ultimate consequences can only lead to one conclusion. The ability—and willingness—to communicate is the single most important personal skill any individual can have. This is particularly true for technical people who elect to pursue their careers in a large organization. With good communication, all things are possible. They may not happen— nothing is guaranteed—but a least the chance is there. Without effective communication, nothing is possible. In fact, opportunity and accomplishment often grind to a frustrating halt.

MEMO WRITING

Memos, by definition, are interoffice communication vehicles. Any document sent between individuals employed by the same organization is considered to be a memorandum or an IOC.

Geography doesn't count. Memos are sent between home office and field office or parent corporation and subsidiary as easily as from individual to individual within the same department. They are the primary *internal* means of task distribution and information exchange in any working environment—large or small.

To a great extent, the memorandum has replaced the business letter. Many individuals, especially in data processing, write only memos and read only memos. The number of IOCs written and distributed grows daily.

This volume, in conjunction with poor quality overall, has created a serious problem in effective memo utilization. Far too many writers are openly skeptical about what they can hope to accomplish in any memorandum. Far too many readers are cynical about the memos they receive, even before they read them. If in-house communication is to work, we must change these attitudes.

Why? Because we're stuck with memorandums. Despite their bad reputation, no organization can function without them.

How? The techniques are here—ways to write only what we must and ways to make what we do write better.

9
Types of Memos

Many people find memo writing difficult because they don't know how to begin. The first step for anyone thinking to himself, "Where do I start?" is a review of the types of interoffice communication.

Memorandums written by data processors can be classified into six categories. Once you understand the characteristics of each, you can match your proposed memo against established definitions. Where your document fits a category description, valid objective and the initial framework for your document are easily determined. All that remains to be done is some solid thinking about your reader(s) and the actual writing.

Careful study of these categories also eliminates unnecessary memorandums. Each designation is a guideline to what is essential in data processing communication and what is not. If the memo you plan to write is not representative of any of the six types, re-evaluate it. With few exceptions, you probably do not need to write at all.

1. Review and Presentation Memos

Initiative. These are assigned memorandums. Management in your area defines a stiuation or problem. They then ask you to review all possibilities and present your viewpoint or recommendations. Objective is established by the requestor. You often modify or refine the original definition, however, based on the results of your investigation.

Reader(s). These documents have varying audiences depending on content. They can be addressed to your management, users, support areas, or department personnel. Where required, informational copies are provided to administrative groups such as interdepartmental committees that set priority or control expenditures. The requestor, if not the primary reader, should receive a copy.

Content. Actual subject matter ranges from complex analysis to simple procedural adjustments. These memos are alway geared to *current* action, however. They are not forecast vehicles. Solutions or suggestions offered are intended for current usage.

Format. Content is arranged from problem or situation as defined to writer-suggested action. In each instance, reader response in the form of a decision, agreement, or completed work is requested by a specific date.

2. Definition and Presentation Memos

Initiative. This memo is always initiated by the writer. Generally, a condition or problem will develop in the context of your job responsibilities that you feel must be documented. This memo type allows you to define the parameters of the situation as you see them. It also is a vehicle for presentation of your proposed solution or any viable alternatives.

Reader(s). These memorandums outline areas of concern recognized only by you. Therefore, they are always made available to your management, either by direct address or by copy. With this one restriction, the audience is the same as for Review and Presentation Memos.

Content. Areas discussed vary from internal crisis to routine work requirements. Most important is a detailed and convincing definition of the situation that prompted you to write. Unless the reader considers your topic as important as you do, he will not implement the solution you present. As with Review and Presentation Memos, any suggestions offered should by useful immediately. These memorandums are not employed for long-range projection.

Format. See Review and Presentation Memos for arrangement of content.

3. Status Reports

Initiation. These reports, written to record progress on specific projects or services, are required documents in most data processing environments. They are prepared at specific time intervals as set by management in each area—weekly, bimonthly, monthly, etc. Some convey only individual status. Others present team, shift, or departmental activity.

Reader(s). The primary reader for a Status Report is the writer's immediate boss. Most Status Reports move upward vertically through administrative levels, undergoing modification at each level. Also, some data processing groups now distribute copies of their Status Reports to user or customer areas.

Content. Information is offered on task completion, current work assignments, and projected allocation of time and other resources. Existing and anticipated problems are documented, usually with suggested solutions.

Format. The traditional sequence in status reporting is chronological—where you've been, where you are, where you're going. This is not, however, necessarily the most effective arrangement. Many managers prefer "bad news first," using Status Reports as a crisis-warning device. In almost every instance, format is prescribed in each individual area, with all Status Reports prepared in one area following the same predetermined format. Some groups have also introduced printed Status Report Forms with associated graphs, time charts, or work flow diagrams.

4. Information Memos

Initiative. These memos are written either to disseminate information or to elicit information you require to complete a specific task. They can be assigned by management or initiated by the writer.

Reader(s). When providing information, copies are sent to all individuals involved in the subject area being discussed. Support or management groups whose personal responsibilities will be affected by reader use of the information are also copied.

In eliciting information, the inquiry is directed to those most familiar with the topic. Examples would be end users, decision-making individuals or groups, and anyone who will be affected by your use of the information once you receive it.

Content. Dissemination of information must satisfy these reader questions— who, what, how, when, where, and why. Examples should be provided, whenever possible. Specialized terminology is carefully defined, according to reader experience and level of comprehension.

Memos eliciting information always contain two elements—what is needed and why the request is important, to the reader as well as the writer.

Format. Information is presented to the reader in straightforward and easily understood sequence. Usually, what is most important to the reader must come first. Questions and other feedback are always encouraged.

Information needed from the reader should be requested by specific questions. Where possible, blanks are provided after each question. The reader can then simply record his reply on your document, make a copy, and return your original memorandum. Response levels go up, and turn-around time is shortened.

The sequence of "what is needed" and "why it's important" varies depending on content and reader attitude. For example, some readers must know "why" before they are motivated to examine the "what" and furnish it. Response is always requested by date.

5. Management Reports

Initiative. These are investigative documents. Writers initiate them to propose action—both current and future—in a specific work situation. They also, however, are often either assigned by management or written in response to user request. Management Reports range in type from short, simple manpower projections to the longer, more complex Feasibility Study or Proposal.

Reader(s). Readers of Management Reports are determined strictly on the basis of need-to-know. The primary reader is most often the individual who must make a decision based on the recommendations as presented. Most Management Reports, however, are distributed on an extensive "information only" list. This list contains the names of anyone who will be affected by or involved in possible end result.

Content. These documents are the major forecast tool of management. They should provide solid information on current business situations, anticipated areas of concern, and suggested future courses of action. Data, analysis of data, and writer recommendations are crucial to reader comprehension. Each should be presented in a way that facilitates intelligent management decisions within a specified time framework.

Format. See Chapter 20, page **178**.

6. Inquiry Response

Initiative. Initiative has been taken by a reader who asks a question or makes a request. The writer's primary responsibility is a *prompt* and useful reply.

Reader(s). The response is directed to the originator of the inquiry, unless he specifies otherwise. Where necessary, copy your management. This is particularly important if your reply is negative. Also, copy any individual or group referenced in your response.

Content. Content is determined to a large extent by the document you receive from your respondent. Answers to his or her questions must be provided, along with any "stage-setting" information necessary to reader understanding and acceptance. If you cannot respond immediately, notify your reader. Give him a date on which he can expect a reply. If you cannot respond adequately or at all, say so, and direct your reader to the proper source.

Format. Arrangement of your response can be simple—anything from answers written on the original inquiry to a brief statement of the information requested. In most instances, arrangement of content should follow that suggested for dissemination of material in Information Memos.

The response to an inquiry can also be complex, however, depending on the size and nature of the request. If a reader expects extensive analysis, your reply becomes a Management Report. If what your reader originally requested is not what he actually requires, your response becomes a Definition and Presentation Memo.

10

Memo Checklist

Four problems stand out in the data processing memorandums I review. I've arranged these in a checklist you can use to evaluate your own interoffice communication. Simply ask yourself, "Did I avoid . . . ."

1. The Sly Fox and the Big Brown Bear

This catch phrase is an apt description of a prevalent, but highly nonproductive, syndrome in business communication. Here's how it goes:

I work for you. I'm on the firing line in our department, deeply involved in actual productivity. Because of my direct experience, I come up with something—a new idea, solution to a problem, whatever. I describe my conclusions in a memorandum. Unfortunately, out of tradition or for some other reason, *you* sign the memo *I* prepared. Generals, of course, only talk to generals. The "Sly Fox" has just moved in on the "Big Brown Bear."

Unfortunately, this long-established custom causes at least three serious problems:

Take me, the employee. Once I realize that anything I write is going to be usurped by you, what is my motivational level on subsequent assignments? Since I'm not receiving credit for new ideas, I stop being creative. I also am now going to write more for your approval than to reach the ultimate reader. The quality, if not the quantity, of my writing goes downhill.

Take you, the manager. We've already discussed the fact that the further one gets in levels of administrative responsibility, the less he know about the details of any project or service. When questions come back to you—and they will come back to you, you signed the memo—you probably will not be able to answer them. Your response can only be, "You'll have to talk to Rändi Smith about that," telling the respondent immediately you did *not* write the memorandum. How does this make you look?

I've actually seen some managers add a tag line saying, "If you have questions, call————." Here, the reader knows from the beginning that the memo was written by someone else. The "Sly Fox" rarely fools anyone.

Take the idea itself. Any reader who finds you don't know what's going on—you can't answer questions, remember—is going to begin to doubt the validity of the entire suggestion or solution. Also, any enthusiasm he may have felt rapidly evaporates as he is passed telephone extension to telephone extension looking for a response.

We've crippled the creativity and motivation of the employee, made the manager look ridiculous, and endangered the acceptance of a good idea. All because we did not keep the communication channels direct.

Certainly, managers must be kept informed. If I work for you, you should have access to what I write. At times, I may even need the "influence" of your position to help sell my idea. We can satisfy both these requirements, however, without the "Sly Fox, Big Brown Bear" routine.

If I write a document, I sign it. You, as the manager, read it and then forward it under a Buck Slip saying: "I have read this. It has my full approval." You sign *only* the Buck Slip.

How do I now feel as an employee? You've afforded me recognition for my efforts. I should be highly motivated to continue such performance. You also have made me responsible for the accuracy of the memo's content. Responsibility encourages excellence.

What about you, the manger? Your Buck Slip demonstrates that you are on top of what is occurring in your area. In fact, you have to look good. Any reader knows if you were not doing your job as an administrator, your people would not be coming up with good ideas.

The idea itself is now protected. Any questions will be directed to me. I know the most about the subject and should be able to field them adequately. Because the reader has direct access to the answers, his initial enthusiasm is maintained. Our department as a whole appears competent and well organized.

We also have probably lessened overall turn-around time. The memo goes out faster, because everyone in the department is not editing prior to distribution. Questions are answered quickly, so reader response should be prompt and positive.

There are other alternatives to "the Sly Fox and the Big Brown Bear." Depending on the circumstances, you and I could prepare a joint memorandum, signed by both. Where your commitment is required—perhaps for reasons of legality—you must sign the memo. Your first sentence, however, should read, "Rändi Smith and I . . . ." This allows you to legitimately pass questions or objections to me. No reader can question my involvement when I was cited in the original document. Your out-front recognition also maintains my incentive.

2. Long repetition of facts with no analysis

This is data processing's well-known Laundry List approach. I believe it's a hang-over from our technical training, where gathering facts and throwing them on a page was accepted format.

Contemporary data processing applications require more. Each writer must take a position. Readers expect analytical and professional judgment from an expert. They often cannot analyze already available data or are unsure of their interpretation. Therefore, they look to the writer for problem definition and a projection of possibilities.

Presenting the results of your investigation also helps elicit a more specific response from your reader. People find it much easier to take potshots at something definite. There's a big difference between

"Here is the information to be provided . . . ."

and

"Here is our suggested report format . . . ."

The content is the same, but its arrangement into detailed examples opens constructive and usually productive dialogue in any problem-solving process.

3. Formula writing

I am not objecting to the use of forms. Carefully designed forms meet many recurring needs in any data processing operation. As long as they are reviewed and perhaps updated, at least on an annual basis, forms simplify and accelerate predefined communication functions.

Formula writing is something else. It prevails for two simple reasons.

One, many technical people do not like to write.

Two, many technical people find themselves dealing repetitiously with the same people and similar situations or problems.

Say we develop a memorandum that works in a particular instance. Should the same circumstances arise again, isn't it a great temptation to go to the file and pull out our once-successful document? Oh, we change the names and the date. We modify a few minor elements to protect either the innocent or the guilty, depending on one's point of view. It is, however, the same memo, isn't it? Readers catch on to this more quickly than you might suppose.

On December 10 of one year, I received exactly the same memorandum from a correspondent that he had sent me the preceeding November 10. Only the name of the month changed. I did not feel, and no other reader would either, that this writer offered me even minimum personal attention.

Formula writing seems an easy solution. It precludes, however, any honest consideration of who we are dealing with and what is required. The tone is strictly one of "standard operating procedure," creating resistance, if not actual reader resentment.

4. Business riddles

What is obvious to us, we tend to assume is equally obvious to our reader. We write as if he were somehow looking over our shoulder, seeing exactly what we see. Business phrasing and stylized formats make it easy to present a statement—crystal-clear to our mind—that is muddied or incomplete to our respondent.

Take this example:

> "New recruitment methods resulted in the filling of 66 percent of outstanding personnel requisitions."

The writer knew what he was saying. Does the reader, however? The reader's most important concern is *how many people were hired.* Unless he knows the number of outstanding personnel requisitions, he can't compute this figure. He knows little more after reading this riddle than he did before. The writer, hiding behind a forest of traditional business words and phrases—percentages, outstanding requisitions—failed to show his reader the important trees. It's much more effective to write:

> "New recruitment methods enabled us to hire 10 people at the following levels . . . . We have 6 positions still open."

Even personalization and the use of examples do not always cure the problem of conventional, yet exasperating, vagueness.

> "Thanks to the vigorous effort of Marie Simpson in Personnel, we supplemented our programming staff by 66%. In fact, three out of every five project employees are new to the department."

If the reader doesn't know the current level of staff, he again can't come up with the one pertinent number—*how many?* Even if he does know, why make him do the arithmetic?

> "Thanks to the vigorous effort of Marie Simpson in Personnel, we hired 15 new programmers."

COMMUNICATION
AND THE DATA
PROCESSING LIFE CYCLE

Why we write, what we write, and how to write—here are specific solutions to these common problems in data processing communication.

Most of the references will be to memorandums, again because most data processors write and distribute more interoffice communication than traditional business letters. I don't want to get hung up on semantics, however. In many organizations, the terms "report" or "study" are used, even though the document is written and distributed as a memorandum. Those data processors who do write business letters are generally conveying the same information their in-house counterpart presents in memo format. Whatever your communication vehicle, the techniques for successful completion remain the same.

Any request for data processing service—DPSR (*D*ata *P*rocessing *S*ervices *R*equest), memo, or telephone call—can, during its life cycle, initiate seven different data processing memorandums. Such requests must be processed internally, no matter what the data processing application, from every step in the development process to all aspects of computer operations. (See Exhibit A.)

Let's take each of the suggested memorandums and examine it individually. What is its relationship to data processing objectives? How can we use it to lighten our workload? Does it build a bridge to our user?

One footnote before we begin. I am not insistent on the names I have given these memos. Every shop in every organization has its own names. My main concern is the opportunity offered by each document for more effective communication and fewer day-to-day hassles.

Call these memorandums whatever you like. The fact you're calling them anything at all will mean you're using them, and *that* is what I'd like.

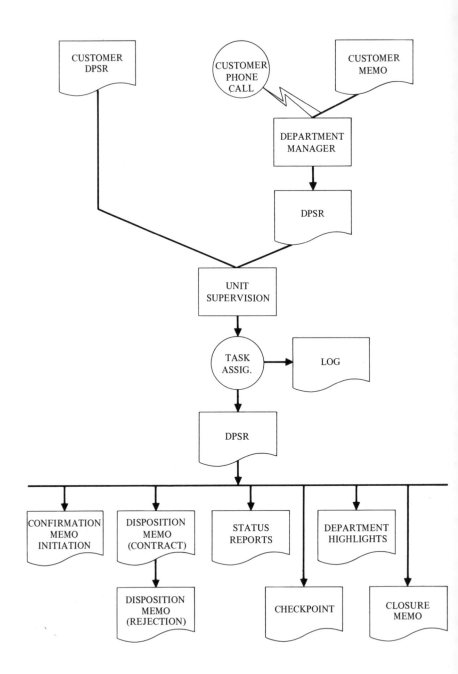

Exhibit A

11
The Confirmation Memo—
Initiation

Confirmation is basically a courtesy vehicle. It is written at the initiation of a development or service effort to establish a valid communication channel between DP and the customer.

Often, we cannot say yes or no to a request promptly upon receipt. We may need time to evaluate. We may not have sufficient information to proceed. Whenever we are unable to make immediate disposition, the Confirmation document is a businesslike and service-oriented response. It reassures the user of our concern and interest, while buying us adequate time for sound professional judgment.

Here are the elements for efficient Confirmation.

1. Acknowledge receipt of the DPSR or request one if the customer request came in other format.

If the request was presented in writing—DPSR, memorandum, or letter—this document affirms receipt. If the request came in verbally—over the telephone, during a discussion, or in a meeting—we can use the Confirmation to ask for the request in *writing*.

Why do we want our user to put his needs on paper? Certainly, a DPSR or memorandum is necessary as written record of the initiation of a request. Even more important, asking someone to write down his requirements often changes the nature of the request. It is one thing for a customer to casually mention something he would like to have during a telephone conversation. It is quite another for him to attempt to spell out what he wants in prose. Require someone to write something down, and he tends to think through his ideas carefully and in greater detail.

2. Give the department control number.

Most data processors keep track of requests by an assigned number designation. In some organizations, it is the DPSR number. In others, it is the PCN (*P*roject *C*ontrol *N*umber) or SCN (*S*ervice *C*ontrol *N*umber). Whatever internal numbering device you use for allocation of time and other resources, be sure your customer knows it. Ask him to use it in all future communication. This ensures that you are both on the same wavelength, simplifying future progress reporting and time and cost accounting. The user may now also charge any necessary allocation of his own personnel and other resources against the same number. This is a great assist to corporate bookkeeping and the only way to accurately determine *overall* costs at completion.

3. Specify any additional information needed to evaluate customer needs.

Requests can come in without sufficient detail. Some users don't know what information we require and so don't provide it. Others assume we know more about their situation than we actually do.

Whenever you receive a vague or incomplete request, use the Confirmation to spell out additional information necessary to your evaluation. Not only will you elicit clarification of this request, you will help your customer learn what information should be included in subsequent requests.

4. Provide department contact.

Responsibility for disposition of a user request is often delegated. A DPSR or customer requisition coming in to the manager of a DP area is generally passed to someone else for processing.

If you are transferring responsibility to another individual, notify your user. Provide the name, title, and telephone extension of the appropriate person to be contacted after Confirmation. This keeps the communication channel direct. Your customer knows who his contact is, what he or she does, and the correct number for immediate access to information or other assistance. Also, you will not receive either written or verbal communication that you do not want and probably could not handle.

5. Ask for the name of the customer liaison.

We are providing a contact in our area. Now we need to know who in the user department will be on tap to answer our questions or help us further. Customers also delegate responsibility. The individual submitting the original request is not always our liaison for the duration of the project or service. Determine the appropriate name, title, and telephone extension to facilitate future contact.

Requesting the name of their liaison is also a subtle way of telling inexperienced or indifferent users that such an assignment must be made in their area.

6. State specific date for report back to customer.

This is what makes any ''stall'' work. Remember, we *can't* answer our user's most important question—''yes or no?'' Providing the date on which we will do so, however, generally means he will wait. Customers who don't have a specific time framework start calling to check on their requests. You can only get away with the response, ''I'm working on it,'' once or twice. After that, the user knows you're *not* working on it. It's buried in your ''when I get around to it'' file.

Realistically determine how much time you require and tell your customer. He now has no reason to telephone you in the interim unless he is providing additional information or has a question.

Don't, however, box yourself in. If you must request additional information from your user, your response date is dependent on receipt of what you require. Let him know this. You could say:

''I will have an answer for you within two weeks of receiving . . . .''
or:
''Please let me have this information by September 28 so I can get back to you by October 5.''

****

Apply these techniques from SIX KEYS TO SUCCESS when writing a Confirmation:

1. Valid assumptions about the reader

The content and length of this document is determined by your knowledge of the customer's experience and comprehension levels. A sophisticated user should provide sufficient information in his initial request. His main concerns are your acknowledgment of his request, the assigned control number, and the date on which he can expect disposition.

Inexperienced or new users require a different approach. They probably did not include all necessary information and may not understand your request for it without careful explanation and/or verbal follow-up. These readers generally require ''stage-setting'' information, such as the proper usage of the internal control number. They also must be provided precise definitions for any jargon or specialized terminology.

2. Brevity

Brevity is, of course, crucial to any effective written communication. Confirmation, however, is where I most often see *content* sacrificed for brevity. Many organizations attempt Confirmation by pre-printed form, eliminating the personalization so necessary to the initiation of a sound working relationship. Such forms curtail helpful explanation to new users. They also imply a "standard operating procedure" approach and lack of service orientation to experienced and inexperienced customers alike.

The Confirmation document can be brief, but it must be comprehensive. Attitudes, understandings—and misunderstandings—established at Confirmation easily linger to complicate things right through to completion.

3. Recognize your customer's need for prompt attention.

Any user submitting a request wants an answer. The longer he waits, the more skeptical he becomes of the response he finally receives.

Most Confirmations are distributed within two working days of receipt of a DPSR or customer requisition. This turn-around time will vary, of course, depending on the size and complexity of the request. Some development areas need more than two days to determine what additional information is necessary.

Whatever the constraints of your environment, however, make the turn-around as brief as possible. Wait too long and your user is already on the telephone or writing follow-up memorandums. Once he feels he must push to get action, no Confirmation can convince him you are *willing* to provide good service.

****

Sample Confirmation Memo—Initiation

The best way to test the opportunities afforded by this document is to write one. Let's say you have received the following request. (See Exhibit B.)

Using scrap paper, actually write a Confirmation Memo in response, conveying the following information:

DPSR NO. EX 1992
PROJECT CONTROL NO. 668
NEEDED FROM CUSTOMER: SAMPLE OF OUTPUT REQUIRED SHOWING FORMAT. NUMBER OF OUTPUT COPIES NEEDED BY USER.
JOHN PARSONS, SYSTEMS SUPERVISOR, WILL FORWARD A PHASE OUTLINE AND COSTS WITHIN ONE WEEK OF RECEIVING THE MATERIAL. HIS TELEPHONE EXT. IS 6618.

DATA PROCESSING SERVICES REQUEST

D.P.S.R. NUMBER	
EX1992	
SYS. CODE	EX. CODE

Project Control
No. 668

NAME OF JOB	TYPE OF REQUEST			
PRODUCT LIABILITY OUTSTANDING LOSSES	☒ NEW	☐ CHG.	☐ CORR.	☐ ONE TIME

EXISTING SYSTEMS AFFECTED	FIRST PROD. DATE DESIRED
☐ YES ☐ NO	September 1, 19XX

ESTIMATED DATE FOR SYSTEM DESIGN PROPOSAL	DUE DATE EACH CYCLE
	September 1, 19XX

PROCESSING CYCLE FREQUENCY

☐ DAILY ☐ WEEKLY ☐ MONTHLY ☐ QUARTERLY ☒ ANNUAL ☐ OTHER

TP USE: ☐ IN HOUSE ☐ NATIONWIDE ☐ DIAL-UP ☐ SCHEDULED

BRIEF DESCRIPTION

(USE ADDITIONAL SHEETS IF NECESSARY. USE THIS SPACE TO EXPLAIN ABOVE ANSWERS SPECIFYING CHANGES IN SCHEDULING RUN TIME, DEVICE USAGE AND REGION SIZES.)

PURPOSE: To supply the Actuarial Department with Outstanding Losses for Product Liability by policy year valued at 3/31/xx.

INPUT: General Liability Outstanding Loss experience date.

PROCESSING:
1. Extract Kind Codes 126, 127 and 426 from Outstanding Loss Cards.
2. Furnish a report to the Actuarial Department.

OUTPUT: Outstanding Loss Listing for Product Liability.

REQUESTER'S NAME M. J. Mitchell	DATE	TITLE Supervisor	
DEPARTMENT Actuarial		TEL. NO.	CONVEYOR
DIVISION DATA PROCESSING CO-ORDINATOR	☐ APPROVED	☐ DISAPPROVED	DATE
OFF. IN CHARGE, DIVISION DATA PROCESSING	☐ APPROVED	☐ DISAPPROVED	DATE

Exhibit B

Of course, you will first have to decide "who" you are dealing with. Is M. J. Mitchell "Michael" or "Mark"? Perhaps she is "Martha"? It doesn't matter what name you pick. Just be sure you are not using only initials. Also, I'm going to ask you to make one major assumption about this user. Mitchell—Mike or Martha—is *new* to data processing.

****

Now that you've completed your Confirmation, evaluate it in light of these considerations:

1. Reader comprehension

Did you link the numbers—either DPSR or PCN—with the name of the request in your Subject heading? Remember, we tend to think in terms of the numbers. Users think of names. In fact, the name should come first for instant reader recognition, helping new users learn to associate the number with the name.

You can even go one step further. If you think your reader may still not know how to use the numbers, simply add a parenthetical phrase to your Subject heading explaining future utilization.

Using both name and number is also important with experienced customers. They may be keeping track of more than one job already in progress and need to immediately connect new job with assigned number.

If you do put both name and numbers in your heading, you can save a first sentence. "We are in receipt of your request for . . . " is totally superfluous. You couldn't use the name in your Subject heading if you hadn't received the request.

2. Reader expectation

Mitchell is looking for a yes or no answer. You can't give it to him. You have, however, taken positive action on his request—you assigned John Parsons. Did you point this out *first* in your content sequence? Not only does it introduce John right from the beginning, but such action assures Mitchell you are taking his request seriously.

3. Request for the output sample

You've asked a *new* user to provide a sample of the output showing format. Most new customers, and some experienced ones, assume that job belongs automatically to DP. Did you include anything with your Confirmation to make the job easier for your reader and his response more productive for you?

You might have enclosed a standard output format sheet. This starts Mitchell on his way, showing him the spaces he has to play with. Be careful, however. The output sheet makes his job simpler, but can complicate yours. Show a user how many spaces are available and he inevitably fills them—not necessarily in the best way for your technical considerations.

You could have included some listings similar in type to what Mitchell needs. Ones, perhaps, that you prepared for other departments. Used as a guideline, these provide graphic illustration of good use of space, headings, etc.

If you had time, you and John Parsons might have come up with a suggested sample on your own. Any reader is more likely to comment specifically on something he can see than he is to create from scratch.

My guess is, however, that you and John will ultimately have to sit down with Mitchell and discuss user requirements. Why not use this document to set up the necessary meeting?

4. The meeting

Many data processors would simply call Mitchell (or have John do so) to ask for a meeting. I do not recommend this for two reasons:

One, you still need the Confirmation to establish the numbers.

Two, no one can come to a meeting prepared to discuss a subject he doesn't understand. Also, Mitchell is probably not the one with the answers. He will have to confer with others—management, end users—in his department. Remember the child's game of Gossip? By the time Mitchell explains the meeting agenda to two or three people, will his version of your request in any way resemble what you originally told him on the telephone?

Use the Confirmation to set up a meeting, specifying time, date, and place. The place, of course, is Mitchell's location, if possible. All the information is there. If he comes to your office, a crucial file or the one person who can answer questions is always missing.

You certainly don't want to ask Mitchell to call John to set up a meeting either. If you must do the work, you retain the initiative. Otherwise, Mitchell is sure to call for a meeting when it is least convenient. Once you say a meeting is necessary, you are not in a good position to then decline or defer the date he selects.

Not only can you set meeting date, time, and place, you can also specify participants. How often have you attended a meeting, only to find someone missing—someone important enough to your objective so that another meeting becomes inevitable? For instance, you certainly want the user liaison present at your meeting. Spell this out. Even when you do not know individual names, you can designate crucial participants by their function. Examples might be end users or decision-making administrators from the customer area.

Of course, your selected date, time, or place may not be convenient to Mitchell, and you would have to allow for this. Ask him to let you know *by a specific date* if he and the others will be able to attend. If you do not ask for a response by date, we all know what occurs. A person calls from the user area minutes before the scheduled meeting to tell you Mitchell is in Bermuda, but so-and-so will substitute. Now, you're into another follow-up meeting situation.

5. Time requirements vs. customer expectations

Suppose Mitchell and his group come to the meeting prepared. They supply you and John Parsons with all the necessary material. What are they going to expect at the conclusion of the meeting? Isn't it an answer from you? Are you going to be able to provide such information? If not, *now* is the time to tell Mitchell that John Parsons will need one week from the date of the meeting to evaluate results and formulate a definite response.

6. Open door

It's possible—even though you provide all the samples and explain the meeting agenda carefully—that Mitchell still won't understand what you require. When do you suppose you will find this out? In my experience, it's at the meeting itself. You spend two to three frustrating hours answering questions. Then Mitchell must have time to get his material together, of course, so you break and schedule yet another meeting.

Elicit any difficulties on the part of your user as early as possible by keeping your door open. Suggest that if he has any questions or wishes to discuss any aspect of the original request, he call John *prior to the meeting.* This—in a nice way—tells your customer you expect him to come to the meeting prepared.

****

It sounds as if we're touching quite a few bases with one document, doesn't it? Let's sequence out our Confirmation and determine if we can accomplish all our objectives with just *one* memorandum and *one* meeting.

> SUBJECT: Product Liability Outstanding Losses DPSR# EX1992, PCN# 668
> (Please use these numbers in all future communication.)

1. I have assigned John Parsons, Systems Supervisor, to your request.

2. John and I would like to meet with you, your liaison and (other necessary participants) on (date) at (time) at (place—user's office, where possible) to discuss—

   A. The number of output copies required.
   B. Output format.
      (See enclosed samples.)

3. If not convenient, call John by (date) to set up alternative.

4. John will require (time framework from date of meeting) to evaluate material and provide detailed response.

5. If you have questions or need assistance, please call John, tel. ext. 6618, prior to the meeting.

6. Thank you.

c: John Parsons

In evaluating this sequence, begin with the customer's viewpoint. I think you can see how this approach immediately conveys to him your personal competency and the efficiency and service orientation of your entire department. Any user—new or experienced—now feels more comfortable with what you expect him to provide. Even more importantly, he can solicit the necessary participation from his people and/or management, assured you are processing his request in a professional and businesslike manner.

Now consider your own frame of reference. This sequence also makes your job easier. Any necessary work activity will be done on your timetable. By making it as easy as possible for your customer to supply what you need, you should receive better information with less overall expenditure of time and effort. With one document, you have broken the frustrating cycle of meetings, telephone conversations, and memorandums so common to the initiation of a new DP project or service.

One further note. Many organizations have an unwritten rule that the individual receiving a request must respond to it. If, however, you do not have this restriction, there is another option. Should you wish to delegate full responsibility and have no further involvement, John Parsons can write the Confirmation. All that changes in our original sequence are the personal references. For example, in element #1, John would write, "(your name) has asked me to handle your request." In element #2, he would say, "*I* would like to meet . . . ," leaving you out of the meeting situation altogether. Of course, the remaining use of his name would become the proper pronoun. Just remember when employing this technique that you are now the one who receives a copy.

12

Disposition Memo
(Acceptance)—The Contract

This document has many names. In some development areas, it is the Systems Contract. In others, it is a required Phase Completion Report. In most operations facilities, it becomes a Service Contract. Whatever its designation, the important thing to remember is that it is a *contract*.

We need to impose some businesslike structures on the function of providing data processing service. Too many serious crises develop because neither the data processors nor the user understand, *from the beginning,* what is going to take place. Too many problems are hell to solve because responsibility was never agreed upon.

The Contract approach, used to accept a customer's request, eliminates the uncomfortable pressures of nebulous or ever-changing user requirements. A Contract involves both the data processor and the user in a sensible exchange of information and effort. For the first time in many organizations, each knows exactly where he stands. Credibility is firmly established and, therefore, easily maintained. Contracts are the only sure cure for our disliked, but longstanding, "fly by the seat of your pants" reputation.

Here are the necessary elements:

1. Be specific in outlining department responsibility.

Spell out, in detail, exactly what you are going to provide. In a development context, this generally takes the form of system specifications. Some Contracts, in fact, cannot be written until after completion of a Feasibility Study, which then becomes a Contract exhibit. In a methods and procedures area, you must document existing procedures or the lack of them prior to outlining new ones. However it is defined, this section of the Contract is a concise presentation of the *what*.

Realize, however, that in describing what you're going to provide, you have only touched on part of the necessary ingredients. We've known for years that the user's commitment is as important to successful completion as our own. How many customers realize this?

We can use the Contract to stipulate the user's obligations. For example, in the development process, the user will have to be around to assist in problem definition. He also will have to participate in the development of test data and be available to evaluate test results. In operations, the user must understand and agree to scheduling. He could be expected to deliver proper input. He usually is responsible for usage and assessment of output, often including error recognition.

Whatever responsibilities exist, clearly explain them—on both sides of the fence.

2. Introduce the person in charge.

We want all communication channels to remain direct. If you are now delegating authority for this project or service to someone else, tell your customer. Provide the name, title, and telephone number of the person he should call with questions, information, or problems. Users deal more easily with a new "chief honcho" whose credentials have been established.

3. Present a phase or task outline with descriptions, time schedule, and estimated cost.

We are now expanding the *what* to include the *when* and the *how much*. For those of you on Project Management or some other phased approach, this is established format. Detail what will occur in each Phase, its associated target dates and estimated cost.

If you are not on a phased approach, you still probably develop Task lists and determine time framework and costs. Some of you may employ the *P*roject *E*valuation *R*eview *T*echnique or PERT. This automated system establishes specific Tasks and the time sequence for each.

In operations areas, the breakdown is usually by Quarter. Scheduling information or whatever objectives are pertinent are provided in three-month segments, again always with estimated cost.

Be sure to include user responsibility in each Phase, Quarter, or Task description, along with the estimated cost of user involvement. We not only want our customer to understand the *what* of his commitment, we want him to realize *when* it will be called due and *how much* the allocation of resources will cost him.

Present the Phases, Tasks, or Quarters in the way you feel your user will most easily understand them. Straight outline format is common. However, I also have seen PERT charts or a flow chart diagram used as graphic illustration.

Careful delineation of the more important milestones is particularly important when your Task or Phase outline is lengthy or complex. For example, on long-range development projects, some data processing groups use PERT within their Phases. This complicated process confuses inexperienced and sophisticated users alike. (It also confounds many data processors.) In such a situation, customers might be better off knowing only the Phases, their target dates, and estimated cost, even though you continue with PERT as an internal control.

4. Explain design freeze.

Design (or Service) Freeze simply tells the user something we have always known and he has, somehow, always missed. If he changes anything about the *what,* the *when* and the *how much* also change.

Notice we are not telling our customer we refuse to change the system specifications, scheduling, or whatever. Final option usually remains his. All we are doing is warning the user that changes do impact time schedule and often escalate the originally estimated cost. Should he insist on modification, now or once the project or service is underway, this advance notice works to our advantage. At least, it is not a surprise to the customer when we then adjust target dates and cost as required.

Design Freeze also assures us the user will carefully evaluate end product as specified in the Contract. If something he needs is not mentioned, he knows he must "speak now" to avoid later expense or critical delay.

5. Anticipate any foreseeable problem areas.

Based on past experience, you often can determine where problems might develop. In operations, it could be hardware delivery. In methods and procedures, it could be forms design or printing delays. In a development context, it could be availability of data or a wait for the completion of another interrelated system.

Whatever the possibilities, now is the time to prepare your customer for future complications. You may even involve him in problem prevention or the formulation of acceptable solutions.

6. Ask for approval of the Contract by the user department and authorization to begin Phase or Task I.

This is an *authorized* document. The user must send us his approval in writing. In some organizations, two copies of the Contract are prepared. Both are signed by the appropriate representative of the data processing area and forwarded to the user. He also signs them, returning one copy to DP and keeping the other for his files.

Consider what we are asking our customer to approve. Of course, we want him to sign-off on the *what,* the *when,* and the *how much.* We also, however, want his signed agreement to his department's responsibilities.

When the Contract approach was first introduced, signatures were not required. I followed several of these unauthorized documents into user areas. Because Contracts are often long and technical in nature, customers were flipping through them, saying casually, "That's great." What they were not doing was reading them. You can imagine the eventual misunderstandings as work progressed. Ask a user to sign-off on a Contract and, at least, he reads.

If you are in a development area, with a phased approach, don't let the "authorization to begin Phase or Task I" throw you. Your Contract is probably called a Phase Completion Report and two different Contracts are written.

Look at the typical 7 Phase/4 Phase outline. (See Exhibit C.)

4 PHASE/7 PHASE
MANAGEMENT PROCESS–SYSTEMS DEVELOPMENT

1.	2.	3.	4.	5.	6.	7.
PROJECT INITIATION	SYSTEM SURVEY	DETAIL ANALYSIS AND DESIGN	PROGRAMMING AND PROCEDURES DEVELOPMENT	SYSTEMS TEST	SYSTEM ACCEPTANCE AND CLOSURE	SHAKE DOWN

| | 1. | | 2. | | 3. | | 4. | |

* PHASE COMPETITION REPORT
** QUALITY ASSURANCE CHECK

Exhibit C

The 7 Phase approach is generally associated with long-range development efforts. If you are using it—or one similar to it—your two Contracts are the Phase Completion Reports for Phase I and Phase III.

The Phase I Contract details only the required effort, time, and money for Phases II and III. In effect, it outlines the resources needed to develop a full-scale Feasibility Study. This careful consideration of the dimensions of System Survey and Detail Design is especially important in cost-conscious organizations. The cost of determining feasibility is a good indicator of total development expense. Where users realize that just completing the initial analysis will be costly, they often scrap the project altogether at the completion of Phase I. These early "no go'' decisions save many data processing groups from investing considerable time and resources unnecessarily.

If requested by the customer, projections of the time and cost for completion of the entire project can be included in the Phase I Contract. The user must understand, however, that these overall figures will probably change once the detailed analysis is complete.

The Phase III Contract (or Completion Report) spells out the *what, when,* and *how much* as established for the remaining development effort from Programming through Shakedown. I think you can see how doing this now, instead of in Phase I, can dramatically improve the accuracy of our estimates. Completion figures are no longer ''guess-timates'' at Project Initiation, but solid conclusions based on knowledge of the requested system's detail design.

Some corporations, on the 7 Phase approach, write their second and final Contract at the end of Phase II. I do not recommend this. Too often, data processors in these organizations find themselves in the uncomfortable position of having to drastically change the numbers after the detail Phase. Their users are geared to the original estimates and generally not receptive to adjustments—especially since the changes usually involve more time and money, not less.

The 4 Phase approach is most effective with smaller projects or systems modification. When using it—or one similar to it—your two Contracts are the Phase Completion Reports for Phase I and Phase II.

Again, the Phase I Contract projects objectives, time, and cost only for the analytical effort. The Phase II Completion Report then covers Programming through System Closure.

Don't, however, lock yourself in.

I have found—with the 4 Phase approach—that many assignments are so minor or simple that writing *two* Contracts is a waste of effort. If you also encounter this situation, you need only write *one* Contract—the Completion Report for Phase I. This single document should meet all your (and your customer's) needs from Analysis through Closure.

7. Establish a distribution list.

Apart from the two authorized copies, this document is an excellent vehicle for keeping people informed. Anyone or any group whose responsibility is referenced or implied in the Contract should receive an ''informational'' copy.

Examples would be:
A. Your liaison in the user area.
B. Any end user other than the requestor.
C. Supporting departments—software specialists, printing services, methods and procedures areas, testing facilities, maintenance groups, etc.
D. A System Review or Quality Assurance Committee, where appropriate.

****

Here are the SIX KEYS TO SUCCESS techniques most pertinent to the Contract:

1. Don't be "iffy."

Being "iffy" in the Contract can cripple the future working relationship between you and your user. Be sure you don't get your customer's hopes up unrealistically. Either you can provide a service or you can't.

Establish your credibility from the beginning. Generalities, constant qualifications, and too many "perhaps" statements can make it sound as though you don't know what you're doing.

Also, don't panic the user unnecessarily. Remember, he has no way to judge the probability factors associated with each of your "ifs."

2. Be specific.

Users cannot evaluate vague proposals. Ambiguous system specifications or indefinite service requirements are confusing.

Be concise. Be specific enough that any possible customer dissatisfaction will surface while the Contract is still open to negotiation. Now is the time for your user to say, "Why can't we?" or "That's not what I meant." Isn't it better to elicit this type of feedback early in the game? Without facts and figures, too many users don't understand what's going on until work is either in progress or completed. Then, instead of questions or suggestions, we get complaints.

3. Watch your jargon.

Keep your Phase or Task outline, time schedule, and estimated costs as jargon-free as possible. The use of specialized terminology can vary, of course, depending on the experience or comprehension levels of your user.

Remember, however, that your customer may not be the only important reader of this document. Contracts (or Completion Reports) can also be distributed to other departments and to groups such as a Systems Review Committee. If this occurs in your organization, you must define your terms, regardless of the sophistication of your user. At least, include a glossary. Tuning out support and management individuals can only mean trouble—both for you and for your customer.

****

Sample Disposition Memo (Acceptance)—the Contract

For you actually to write a sample Contract at this point would be difficult, if not impossible. These documents are often lengthy and contain far too much technical detail to be productively constructed in a hypothetical situation.

You can, however, determine your understanding of the Contract approach by role-playing as if you were the recipient. Once you are able to "think as your reader will think," any Contract you prepare should be comprehensive and workable.

In our Sample Confirmation, you asked the user, Mitchell, to meet with you and John Parsons. Let's assume this meeting was held and the necessary additional information obtained. John now composes a System Contract or Phase I Completion Report as follows:

DPSR ACCEPTED.

DEVELOPMENT PHASES: (PERSON DAYS @ $100, MACHINE HOURS @ $300)

PHASE II	SYSTEM SURVEY— ANALYSIS & DESIGN	5/29	15 PERSON DAYS	$1,500.00
PHASE III	PROGRAMMING & PROCEDURES DEVELOPMENT— SYSTEMS TEST	7/8	19.8 PERSON DAYS 8 MACHINE HOURS	1,980.00 2,400.00
PHASE IV	SYSTEM ACCEPTANCE & CLOSURE	7/26	4 PERSON DAYS	400.00
				$6,280.00

BARBARA DICOCCO WILL COORDINATE THE PROJECT.

SYSTEM WILL REQUIRE A DEDICATED (FOR YOUR USE ONLY) ON-LINE PRINTER AT A COST OF $800.

In evaluating this material, view what John has provided as if you were Mitchell. Consider carefully what he has told you from a *customer's* standpoint. Would you then give John the sign-off he needs?

You should have decided not to give John's Contract your approval. A simple rundown of the crucial elements *what, when,* and *how much* explains why.

1. What

"DPSR accepted" is certainly not specific enough either for customer evaluation of proposed end result or delineation of DP's and the user's respective commitments. John should have provided some projection of system specifications, perhaps in the form of an attached Feasibility Study. This would have allowed you, as the customer, to determine whether what John plans to produce is what you anticipate receiving. He also has failed completely to spell out user commitment. You, as Mitchell, can't possibly agree to responsibility that has not been defined.

Look also at the description of the activity planned for each Phase. John has determined his own Task outline. Again, however, he has omitted any required customer participation in each Phase. As the user, you not only do not know for sure *what* you will be expected to do, you don't know where your commitment fits in the overall work assignment.

2. When

Consider the date associated with each Phase. As a data processor, John could easily be thinking of them as "start" dates for each Task. As the customer, however, you are much more likely to see them as absolute "completion" dates. Such misunderstanding can only be avoided if John provides *two* dates for each Phase—"start" date and "stop" date. Users as well as data processors have always found it difficult to work solely with lapsed time or the number of person days required. By showing both dates, John would enable everyone to see the time or calendar framework occupied by each Phase activity.

Another date is also missing from John's Contract. For a customer, wouldn't the proposed date of your first production run be of critical importance? The estimated production or implementation date of any system should be included. How else can a user adequately assure effective utilization of a system as soon as it becomes available to him?

3. How much

John has told you the DP costs for each Phase and the overall development cost as currently estimated. There are, however, other costs you, as a customer, must consider.

As we mentioned in our discussion of the *what*, John did not specify user commitment, either across-the-board or by Phase. Since he did not provide this information, no customer can accurately determine the cost to his department or company of meeting his responsibilities. Surely, any allocation of people or other resources from the user area will cost. The crucial question—and it must be answered before the customer makes any commitment—is exactly *how much*.

Also, in many organizations, customer expense does not end with the development effort. John should have anticipated (and estimated) your annual cost in operating the system once it's in production. The clue that this vital figure is missing lies in his final statement.
SYSTEM WILL REQUIRE A DEDICATED (FOR YOUR USE ONLY) ON-LINE PRINTER AT A COST OF $800.
Presented in such a manner, that $800 appears to be a one-shot expenditure. We know it is more likely a monthly bill. This, and any other continuing costs, must be clearly expressed before the user finds himself obligated for a system he cannot afford to maintain.

Just as an aside, there is an additional problem with this element in the Sample

Contract. If you looked carefully at Mitchell's DPSR, you will remember that the original request was for an *annual* system. No annual system should require a dedicated printer, so obviously something is wrong with John's total analysis, and he will soon be on the street.

4. Delegation of responsibility

Apart from the *what, when,* and *how much,* there are some other questions you—as Mitchell—might have asked. One is "Who is Barbara Di-Cocco?" You have been dealing directly with John Parsons and his boss. Now, you suddenly find your project in the hands of someone else.

John should have introduced Barbara and established her credentials. Certainly, her title or position would have helped the customer understand her function or why she is now taking over. John also needs to keep all communication channels direct by including Barbara's telephone number or internal extension. At the least, this would keep him from receiving calls he either cannot or will not handle himself.

5. Customer comprehension

John did define his terminology—"DEDICATED (FOR YOUR USE ONLY) ON-LINE PRINTER." He also presented his planned Tasks in an easily understood outline format. He did not, however, explain the most often misunderstood aspect of any Contract—the Design (or Service) Freeze.

You may have been tempted to sign-off on John's document simply because he omitted the entire "Freeze" concept. He has locked himself into the *when* and *how much,* while his customer is left free to change anything about the *what.* Without an explanation of the consequences of such action or how Design Freeze works, John is asking for trouble both now and in the future.

One, no user will take the Contract specifications too seriously, particularly if they are complex and would take effort to read and understand. Why do so when he can—to his way of thinking—change anything he doesn't like at some later date. John is not going to elicit any meaningful feedback from his customer because his definition of the *what* probably will not be carefully read.

Two, once the user does wish to institute changes, he will not be prepared for John's insistence on a re-evaluation of the *when* and the *how much.* He may even refuse to consider any adjustment and try to hold John to his original —and now impossible—estimates.

6. Customer decision

Actually, the primary reason for not providing John with signed approval of his Contract is that he didn't ask you for it. His entire document reads as a courtesy vehicle, requiring no action from you whatsoever.

Of course, John must ask for your sign-off, either directly or by including a signature line, and he should ask for it by a specific date.

****

The following document is a good example of an actual Systems Contract. In reading it, be sure to note the following:

1. The request for approval by date *in the beginning,* in the second paragraph of the SUMMARY. This politely informs the reader that without authorization by the date specified, all bets are off and estimates of time and cost will probably no longer be valid.
2. The detailed presentation of user commitment, by date and often by individual.
3. The introduction of the Design Freeze in the next-to-last paragraph.
4. The anticipated distribution list.

Do not be put off if the level of technicality in this document is way above the current sophistication of your customers. Detail provided in any Contract is strictly determined by the writer's assumption about his reader(s). A Contract can be as simple (remember our practice Sample) or as complex as you elect to make it.

Also, although exhibits are referenced throughout the document, they are not included with the example. Reviewing the actual exhibits associated with this Contract would probably be meaningless to you. Please do note, however, the subject areas the writer of this Contract has chosen to clarify with exhibits. This, in addition to the good use of "interruption" technique, gives you some excellent guidelines for the proper use of illustrative material in a Contract situation.

Sample Systems Contract

TO: John Green, Manager, Customer Area or Company
FROM: Susan Feiglein, Sr. Analyst/Programmer, DP Department or Company
DATE: October 3, 19XX
SUBJECT: IAS Compare—Program P78987 & P78988
        Systems Contract or Phase III Completion Report

At your request, we conducted a Feasibility Study of the IAS Compare programs.

SUMMARY:
Our analysis shows the programming support for this project will cost approximately $6,010.00 and take 43 person days. The personnel cost is $4,300.00 and the computer cost is $1,710.00. (See attachment 1 for detailed breakdown.)
These costs, person day estimates and an ETA of December 3, are realistic if we receive your approval no later than October 11.

DISCUSSION:

This job (J78926) is divided into two steps. (See exhibit 1 for basic job flow.)

Step 1 is the IAS Compare program (P78987). It will consist of criteria outlined in the original DPSR with the following:

A. There will be two additional input files:
 1. IAS Compare Parameter card. The starting and ending policy number prefixes will be in IAS format. (See exhibit 2.)
 2. The suspense file (copy record (D742NBMR) will be sequentially searched when a policy number is not found on the IAS file. If the policy number is found on the suspense file, a missing record error will not be produced for the IAS record.

B. The output files for step 1 are:
 1. Missing Records Error report. (See exhibit 4.)
 In addition to this report, we will produce an overnight inquiry transaction record for each of the other files. (See exhibit 5.)
 Peggy Quiros said their area would manually check the six specific edit fields on these inquiry transactions. They will also correct the missing record condition.
 2. Edit Error transaction records. (See exhibit 3.)
 Positions 1 & 2 of these records is the report number. This field corresponds to the specific edit fields listed on the IAS Compare parameter card. (See exhibit 2.)
 Positions 3 through 13 contain the IAS policy number. Preceding each edit field, in these records, is an error indicator. This indicator will flag the field in error in the Edit Error report. (See exhibit 6.)
 3. A turnaround image transaction will be produced for each file for all error conditions. (See exhibit 5.)

The IAS master file will be used as the base file in the comparison of the three files.

Step 2 is the IAS Sort/Format Edit Errors reports program (P78988). This step takes the edit error transactions for step 1 and sorts them in ascending sequence by policy number within report code. It then produces the six Edit Error reports, written on magnetic tape, and dumped at end of job on the model 30 using the CUA V utility programs. (See exhibit 6.)

As discussed with Mark McCall on 9/25, the Premium Anniversary Date edit will be dropped from the IAS compare. He also said the Pension Trust Key Number edit may be dropped and he will get back to us when the decision is made.

As discussed with Jackie Ensrud on 10/5, there are copy records for the IAS master record (D711MST), Status file master record (D700BREC), and the suspense file master record (D742NBMR) on the Life CMS copy library. The only copy record missing was the Name/Address master record (D704MS1). I contacted Claire Evans about this record and she agreed to have a copy of the current Name/Address master record punched. We will be able to compile and do some preliminary testing on CMS.

As we agreed on 9/21, your area will provide us with the following:

1. Test data for the IAS master file and Name/Address file by 10/20.
2. Pan-Valet compile and link JCL for LDP departmental procedures by 10/23.
3. The adpac extract program by 10/23. Fred Sigmund suggested we copy and edit this to create a test Status file.
4. Example of Job Documentation for LDP by 10/23.
5. Call statements and parameters needed for the following modules by 10/24:
   A. M70047
   B. M79902
   C. P78001
6. Marcia Allison said she would provide a current set of reel numbers for the suspense file by 10/24. We will use these for testing. She is also checking on the policy number prefix and suffix values for the suspense file, and what the suspense file billing status code values are or how they are generated.

Some additional information which I will need by 10/25 to test the programs:

1. File identifications for the master files and report files.
2. Constants to be used for overnight inquiries:
   A. IAS Inquiry—Dept/Clerk Code (See exhibit 5A.)
   B. Name/Address Inquiry—Dept. No. & Init. (See exhibit 5B.)
   C. Status Inquiry—Alpha. char. for column 2 (See exhibit 5C.)
3. CMS ID to compile, load and test programs.

Any changes to the DPSR or the above will extend the person day, ETA and cost estimates.

If you have any questions regarding this memorandum or the assignment, please contact me immediately on extension 5516.

Sign-off copies: Manager, DP Area or Company
                        Manager, Customer Area or Company
Informational copies: Liaison, Customer Area or Company
                        Ultimate Users (if applicable)
                        Supporting Departments—DP and Customer
                        Individuals mentioned by name in Contract
                        Systems Review Committee (if applicable)

13

Disposition Memo
(Rejection)—Saying No

Our responsibility as data processors includes the unpleasant task of rejection. We are the ones who must speak out when a request is not technically feasible, when target dates are unreasonable, where a system cannot be cost-justified, where scheduling is impossible.

Most data processors, however, rarely get out a flat *no*. Complicating our job is the fact that final option generally still rests with the user. If he elects to go with a request, in spite of our negative analytical or administrative conclusions, we can wind up doing it anyway. Many of our *rejection* documents seem to be written to convince a customer either to modify his requirements or to postpone his entire request.

Why then is this document called "saying no"? If we have to soft-pedal the minus factors, is it a rejection? I think it is. Consider the user's viewpoint. He made a specific request. Any response that changes or defers that request is going to be read as a no. Whether you definitely veto or write to neutralize the negative aspects of a request, you can expect reader resistance. This is what makes the Disposition (Rejection) situation so difficult.

We can't, however, back off. As the experts, we are usually the only ones who can adequately evaluate a data processing request. Even in organizations where customers do override the data processing viewpoint, our conclusions should be documented. Two reasons:

One, responsibility for later failure or exorbitant time and cost can't be dumped on us.

Two, sooner or later, the end result should convince users and management alike. They'll realize the effort, time, and money they can save by accepting our professional evaulation from the beginning.

Here are the important elements for successful rejection:

1. State decision honestly. Express sincere regret, where appropriate.

We know the bad news must come first. Any customer receiving this document expects an answer to his question, "yes or no?" If your negative response is buried, he'll start skimming—often missing any good news you may have or the explanation for your negative reply.

I don't suggest anything as blunt as a Subject heading beginning, "Refusal of your request for . . . ." Your user would probably be on the telephone before he even read your first paragraph.

Nor am I suggesting printing NO in block letters on a Buck Slip and returning that. The user response to such a reply is easily anticipated.

Instead, consider your reader's mental attitude. If you are sorry you cannot agree to or provide what your customer requested, there's a great deal to be gained by telling him so. An expression of genuine regret is acceptable and effective in any Rejection communication, particularly if the no is final. You could begin:

"I'm sorry, Mike, but we can't . . . ."

Do not use this approach, however, if you are uncomfortable with it. If you personally are ill-at-ease with such statements, or you are *not* sorry, skip it. Otherwise, you will sound as uncomfortable as you feel, causing the user to doubt your sincerity and good intentions.

2. Demonstrate the thoroughness of your investigation. Give reasons for your negative response.

When anyone says no to you, what is your immediate mental question? Isn't it "why?" In order to avoid sounding arbitrary in any negative document, we must give reasons for our decision.

At one time in business communication, explanations were rarely provided. The attitude was, "What is, *is*—and that should be good enough." It never was.

Customers need to understand our rationale for any negative response. This helps them both to accept it more easily this time and to avoid making unrealistic requests in the future.

We also must ensure that our user knows we painstakingly considered his request prior to rejecting or modifying it. No reason for a negative reply appears valid unless we demonstrate that it is a conclusion based on thorough investigation.

For example, in a development context, we often cannot legitimately reject until we complete an initial analysis. In some instances, we must complete the same full-scale Feasibility Study that we prepared prior to accepting a request with the Systems Contract. In an operations area, the impact of a new request on established commitments certainly must be reviewed to determine its practicality.

Whatever investigative effort led to your negative decision, allow your customer to see it. Outline the results of your initial analysis. Include a copy of your

Feasibility Study. Attach a current schedule. This display of examination and research works to your advantage in at least two ways:

One, it shows the user you took his request seriously enough to evaluate it carefully. He is assured you explored every possible means of giving him what he needs.

Two, it lends credence and authority to the reasons given for your negative response. Decision-making individuals in many organizations automatically assume DP's reasons for saying no are a CYA smokescreen of improvisation and fabrication. Now, each reason is shown to be solid fact derived through analytical or administrative inquiry.

3. Recognize customer need. Play up the positive.

We all know what happens when a user discounts our no. Customers consistently rewrite refused requests and resubmit them, either to a different individual at the same level or up one administrative rank. The explanation most users give me for this confusing and nonproductive practice is their belief that the original recipient did not understand their problem. The reasoning goes something like this: "If he had understood how much I needed . . . , he would have provided it."

Write to show your customer you *know* he has a problem. Where possible, emphasize any good aspects evident in his proposed end result. This is especially necessary where you can help your user only if he will agree to modify or postpone his original requirements. Any user who feels his request was denied because you failed to acknowledge its importance will simply try someone else. Any reader who believes your refusal was caused by the way he asked, will rewrite and hit you again.

Reaffirming your understanding of the customer's needs also is an excellent lead-in to any alternatives you may present.

> "I know you're pressed for this data, Mike, and I'd like to help. Perhaps we could . . . ."

It convinces him you are trying to do all you can to provide essential service.

4. Offer viable alternatives.

Rejection is the one communication vehicle in which we actively pass initiative back to our respondent. The problem is his and he must proceed, based on the information and restrictions we've identified.

We don't, however, leave anyone out in the cold.

Where you have turned up alternatives—automated or manual—that will enable your user to obtain all or part of what he requires, outline them. Of course, the decision to accept or reject such substitutes is still his, so be convincing.

Where you must defer a request, be alert to possible interim solutions. Most customers are sophisticated enough to know about borrowing time or getting at least partial data from someone else's file. In fact, customers faced with a postponement seem to have one common question: "What am I supposed to do in the meantime?" Answering this in your original Rejection document again strengthens the thoroughness of your investigative effort. Also, where you do have solid interim solutions, it's easier for your user to live with the delay. In many instances, a good interim solution may even become the *permanent* solution, saving everyone unnecessary additional effort.

One caution. Suppose you did not find any viable alternatives or interim solutions? The request just won't fly—at least as presented. Alternatives still must be mentioned. Leave them out and the user does not assume there weren't any. He assumes you didn't look for them. Reassure your customer that you touched all the bases in trying to meet his needs.

"My investigation did not turn up any alternative (interim) way you can obtain this data. However, John and I will be glad to discuss anything *you* come up with."

This approach places all responsibility for further investigation of alternatives where it belongs—in the user area. Your door, however, is still wide open. Also, by encouraging the customer to respond specifically, you should elicit solid suggestions rather than vague quarreling with your decision.

5. Offer future help and encourage future requests.

Most of us work with the same users on a continuing basis. We can't afford to have our negative decisions generate bad feelings. Recognize that saying no can discourage future requests. Realize that an inflexible attitude can keep a customer from seeking help until his problem has become a crisis.

Encourage the opposite. State your willingness to help where you can. Demonstrate that each request is *new,* no matter what your reaction to the one that preceded it. Remember, you probably will be working with this user anyway. The more cooperative your attitude, the better his response.

****

Here are the techniques from SIX KEYS TO SUCCESS necessary to an effective Rejection document:

1. Avoid clichés, safe thoughts, and worn-out phrases.

I'm sure you can see how such expressions create a poor tone, especially when you must present a negative viewpoint. Using trite or cute phrases to express regret or explain a no only makes you sound insincere or sarcastic or both.

2. Be specific—both in reasons "why not" and in presenting alternatives.

Generalities are never convincing. In telling someone why something cannot be done, provide enough detail to ensure understanding and acceptance.

For example, I once saw the manager of a development area postpone a user request because he "lacked sufficient manpower." Unfortunately, the manager of the requesting department wandered through the DP section about two weeks later, only to see a group of programming trainees working on COBOL P.I. (programmed instruction). He immediately returned to his desk and called the data processing manager. He demanded to know how come DP had people with time to play around with little green books and yet didn't have people to provide badly needed services.

Now you and I know that the programmer trainees probably couldn't have handled the user request. Customers, however, don't understand the various specializations and experience levels in data processing. To them, a warm body is a functioning body—one that should be doing what they require.

The manager of the development department should have recognized this. He could have told the user, in the first place, that he didn't have people available *with sufficient experience* to do the job properly. This would have helped educate the customer. It also would have told him his request was a good one, and we wanted to put our best people on it. (What user doesn't like to hear that?) Now, he's willing to wait.

When presenting alternatives, outline each with enough detail so your user can visualize overall end result. Customers accept something other than their original request only when they understand what the alternative can do for them and why you presented it. Be sure to include the *when* and the *how much*. No user wants to be sold on an alternative, only to find it's too time-consuming or too costly.

3. Watch out for Red Flag words.

Use these in a Rejection document and you're guaranteed a sour response from any reader. The worst offender is *priority*. You might review its use and other words of this type on page 52.

****

Sample Disposition Memo (Rejection)—Saying No

John Parsons has reviewed the material provided by Mitchell at your meeting. His determination of system requirements and his projection of the development effort required has led him to the following conclusions:

DP IS UNABLE TO MEET MITCHELL'S ORIGINALLY REQUESTED PRODUC-
TION DATE OF SEPTEMBER 1, 19XX.

THE DATE CANNOT BE MET BECAUSE DP DOES NOT CURRENTLY HAVE
THE NECESSARY PEOPLE AVAILABLE.

A PRODUCTION DATE OF SEPTEMBER 1, 19XY IS AVAILABLE.

Play John's role. Write a Disposition Memo (Rejection) to Mitchell explaining
the negative decision and possible alternative. You are suggesting that an annual
system be postponed one year.

****

Now, assess your success in saying no by considering Mitchell's point of view and
your own objectives.

1. The decision

Did you put the bad news first? Mitchell is looking for a definite response and will
probably start skimming if you attempt to bury your no. A good technique here is to
focus on the *one* aspect of the request that is preventing acceptance. A totally
different reader reaction is evoked by

"I'm sorry, Mitch, but we can't meet your anticipated production date."

than by a statement denying the entire request.

2. Your investigation

You cannot legitimately tell a user you do not have the necessary people unless you
can tell him *how many* people his request will require. Mitchell not only needs to
know how many people, but you should have specified their level (title) and the
time demanded to do the job. Two reasons:

One, if you cannot provide such specifics, you haven't done your homework
and your negative response will appear casual and arbitrary.

Two, you are preparing to offer Mitchell an alternative production date. How
solid is that second date going to appear if you don't know what his request will
involve? The user is bound to wonder how you came up with your alternative.
Unless you document its basis, he's likely to conclude you pulled it out of thin air
to stall him.

3. Customer motivation

Did you acknowledge Mitchell's needs? Remember, most rejected requests are resubmitted because the user feels DP did not *understand* the situation prompting his request. Recognition of the customer's position assures him of your comprehension. It also is an excellent lead-in to your alternative in that it emphasizes your desire to help the user meet his important objectives.

4. Presentation of alternatives

How many dates did you present? Did you simply offer Mitchell a new production date of September 1, 19XY? As we discussed in the Contract situation, it is crucial to always provide *two* dates, affording the reader a sense of time framework. Now, I am not suggesting you could state categorically—this far in advance—that the necessary personnel will be available April 6, 19XY to begin Mitchell's request. You must, however, have some idea of when these people will be freed up or you could not validly have established the September 1, 19XY target. Spelling out an approximate start date such as

"I should have these people available about the middle of April . . . ."

again demonstrates the thoroughness of your investigation. It shows your customer good management in your area and helps him recognize your time constraints.

Also, in presenting your alternative, did you mention interim solutions? Remember, you are moving a production date a full year. Even if there is no possible interim action, Mitchell should be assured you at least looked for some. In addition, stating that your review of Mitchell's request did not turn up any interim solutions works to *your* advantage:

One, it again substantiates the extent of your investigative effort.

Two, it strengthens the alternative you present by limiting Mitchell's choices from the beginning.

Three, the initiative for further evaluation and suggestions is passed squarely back to the customer—where it belongs. It is *his* problem.

5. Reader action

Once you presented your alternative, you should have asked for the customer's response by a specific date. With a full year involved, Mitchell will feel no pressure to make a decision unless you set a time limitation. It would help if you also gave your user a motive of self-interest for not taking too long to consider your alternative—scheduling considerations or projected work assignments, for example.

You need a decision. You want Mitchell to agree to your alternative date *now,* so you can write a Systems Contract and get it signed. This allows you to plan your work more efficiently. It also prevents future hassle.

Think about your past experience. If you let a user sit around for months discussing and rehashing a request, what usually happens to the initial requirements? What began as a simple DPSR gets every conceivable bell and whistle attached to it, turning into a complete dog-and-pony show. If you wait until April to get Mitchell committed, you are likely to find that the request has now changed so you can't possibly meet the September 19XY deadline. You will have moved a production date one full year, only to then blow the second date. How must this look to the user?

The only way to protect yourself in such a situation is to elicit an immediate answer from your customer and then obtain a signed Contract. Now, the Design Freeze concept is in effect. Mitchell and his people may still change their minds as to the *what* between now and April. You, however, are in a good position to then go to them with necessary adjustments to the *when* (in this case, September 1, 19-XY), and the *how much*.

One caution. Forecasting the *how much* this far in advance could be a problem. Your actual costs may indeed escalate over this long a period of time. The possibility of increased cost once work actually begins should therefore be a potential problem area identified in the ''problem'' section of your Contract.

6. Diary

Whenever you must put off a customer's request more than three months, I recommend the ''diary'' technique. Simply tell your reader you will diary his request and get back to him on a specific date to review the situation. This forestalls the reader response of ''How do I get first on your list if anything changes?'' It eliminates check-up calls from the user over the duration of the postponement. Recognize, however, that a ''diary'' is a commitment. If you do tell a reader you are diarying his request, pull your calendar over immediately and do so. Few gaffes destroy credibility faster than a promised follow-up that never occurs.

In this instance, the ''diary'' works greatly to your advantage:

One, you can end your document on a positive note by offering your continued involvement with the user's request.

Two, your user finds it easier to live with the postponement as he is no longer worried over his request getting lost in DP's constant realignment of schedules.

On January 4, 19XY (or whatever date you specified), you make the telephone call. Probably, nothing will have changed—you still plan to begin in April to get Mitchell up and running September 1, 19XY. The file is open on your desk, however, and you can review the proposed arrangements easily and on your own terms. Imagine how professional and organized you and your entire area appear to a concerned user.

Go one step further. Once you've discussed the situation from your side, ask Mitchell how things look from his side. My guess is that nine times out of ten, he will say something like, ''You know, we were talking the other day and we wondered—while we're at it—if we couldn't also . . . .'' You now know the original request is not going to be the actual assignment, and you've found out while you still have some lead time. You can get an analyst over to Mitchell's area and find out what's been changed. You can ask Mitchell to put his thoughts on paper. Whatever action you take, you have room to maneuver and perhaps still preserve the September 1, 19XY date *in spite* of the customer's revisions. Wait until your proposed start date in April, and this kind of management anticipation is rarely possible.

****

Let's sequence out an effective Disposition Memo—(Rejection) for our sample situation.

SUBJECT: Request for Product Liability Outstanding Losses DPSR# EX1992, PCN# 668
(date of meeting, if one took place)

1. (decision) I'm sorry, Mitch, but we cannot meet your originally requested production date.

2. (reason) Your request will require two systems analysts and five programmers, taking 120 person days to complete. These people are simply not available at this time. (Give reason where appropriate.)

3. (recognize customer need) I know you need this data and would like to help . . . .

4. (alternative) I should have these people available by the middle of April to get you into production by September 1, 19XY.

5. (interim solution or pass initiative) My investigation did not show any way you could obtain the necessary information in the interim, but I would be happy to discuss any suggestions you may have.

6. (approval) Please let me have your response by (date) in order to ensure assignment of these people to your project on our 19XY schedule.

7. (diary) As soon as I receive your approval for the alternative date, I will diary your request and get back to you January 4, 19XY to review the situation.

c: John's boss
Customer liaison
(meeting participants, if required)

This approach incorporates some highly successful features. For example, the use of the phrase "Request for" in the Subject heading suggests (through tone alone) that the request is still pending. It also is important to include the number assignment even in a rejection situation. The time involved in determining your negative response must still be charged to something. Beyond that, if Mitchell accepts your alternative, the request is easily continued under the original numbers. How often does a request wind up with a different number designation following each change or postponement? This assigning of a new number with each alteration has often made it impossible to trace effectively the total cost or time commitment associated with any project or service.

It is also a good idea for John Parsons—who would write the memorandum in our example—to copy his boss. Should Mitchell, for any reason, be dissatisfied with John's no, he will likely move up one level. Certainly, John does not want his boss to give the customer a different reason for the postponement or a different alternative date. Should this occur, there is only one way to square things with the customer. John will wind up doing Mitchell's request by his *original* date. In order to do so, unfortunately, he must pull people off other assignments. His other work will be thrown off schedule and probably go over cost.

There is another reason for John's copying his boss. If Mitchell sees John's boss on the copy list, he knows the decision presented represents a departmental judgment. He recognizes, in most instances, that it will do him no good to carry his wishes one level higher.

The one individual John would never copy—unless he or she had been present at the initial meeting—is Mitchell's boss. To go over your respondent's head—particularly with a no—is a deliberate sandbag, and any reader will resent it as such. John would, in effect, be saying to Mitchell that he lacked the authority to deal directly. If you employ this technique, your readers will bypass you on every future request, automatically initiating all subsequent communication up one administrative level. Where you have to do the work, it's to your advantage to ensure that you will be a part of any discussion or negotiation.

14

The Weekly Status Report

The Status Report is perhaps data processing's least favorite document. We have traditionally resisted all aspects of the "Big Brother is watching" approach to time management. We feel, perhaps rightly, that much data processing effort—particularly the creative aspects—cannot be strictly accounted for. This attitude is reflected in the way we report status. In fact, most of the Status Reports I review are total "fudge." One good example is the "95% complete" routine. I've known systems that were 95% complete for three full years.

One reason we dislike the Status Report as intensely as we do is we have lost sight of its original objective. The Status Report was never intended to be strictly a time allocation device. The ability to keep track of our time is actually a by-product of the progress-reporting process.

The Status Report was developed as a vehicle for vertical communication upward through administrative levels. It is the only solution to our problem of data processing management's exclusion from the technical firing line. It doesn't matter how skilled any administrator may be. No one can operate in a void. Unless valid information moves up, poor management decisions are going to come down. How can we expect anyone adequately to judge either work situations or individual performance when he only has access to incomplete or inaccurate information? The same applies to dissemination of necessary information throughout a department. How can our boss keep us informed when he or she is not?

A user once told me—only half-jokingly—that data processors don't talk to each other except at lunch. He may be right.

One department I visited was divided into three sections—analysts, programmers, and a technical unit. Based on decisions reached by the analysts, the tech unit elected to purchase a particular type of CRT (*C*athode *R*ay *T*ube or terminal). This information went up to DP management, over to the programmers, and out to the user.

120

Three weeks later, the technical unit changed its mind. The user was notified. Guess who wasn't?

The substitution did not go up, and it didn't reach the programmers. Two months later, when they came down to the wire (literally)—coding sheets in hand—what do you suppose happened? *Nothing* happened, unfortunately. How would you like to be the supervisor of that technical unit, who is now on the street? This situation always makes me think of the word *compatible*. It should apply to people as well as hardware.

These elements will help Status Reports bridge such gaps:

1. Detail accomplishments during the time span.

Of course, we must provide information about our activities. Don't overdo it, however. Each of us has some time spans where we don't complete anything of significance—a Phase or Task, for example. This doesn't mean we aren't doing our job. We are. It does mean we have little that's concrete to report.

If you don't have a specific achievement to document, simply record your time and get out. Any of you who must read Status Reports as well as write them, know how tedious it is to plow through the Great American Novel once a week.

My rule of thumb is this. Only detail those accomplishments that will have an impact on where you or your people are going in the subsequent time span. If no such event occurred, resist fiction or editorializing. You don't have to submit a lengthy Status Report to prove you're working.

2. Forecast objectives for the forthcoming time span.

Again, we must employ the management technique of anticipation. Not only should we identify specific goals, we should convey the domino relationship between what we've done and where we're going. Often this is a simple matter of explaining *why* we're doing something as well as what we plan to do.

As with detailing past accomplishments, however, forecasting future objectives can get out of hand. If you do not have a milestone coming up in the next time interval, say so—without copious discussion.

3. Discuss outstanding and foreseeable problem areas. Include possible solutions.

No one wants to be the bearer of bad news. Everyone wants the image of a competent, autonomous problem-solver. As a result, too many data processing managers find themselves in a continual crisis environment. They fight one brush fire after another—most of which could have been avoided if someone had spoken up sooner.

We all know how it goes. Suppose you and I work in the same department. We are both first line supervisors working for Barbara DiCocco. In three weeks, your group expects to pick up results from my team and go with them. I'm Phase III. You're Phase IV.

Now, I'm a good first line supervisor, and I know my unit is slipping. Our target is jeopardized. Yet, am I likely to go to Barbara with this bad news? Probably not. I have three weeks in which to pass a miracle. I could get lucky and get hit by a truck. I'm going to prepare my Weekly Status Report saying: "I put in my time. My people put in their time. We're doing fine."

Another week goes by. Now, we're really behind. Remember, however, I still have two weeks. I could get kidnapped or *something*. Again, I write my Weekly Status Report. Again, I stick to my story: "I'm now putting in overtime. My people are putting in overtime. We're 95% complete."

When am I going to go to Barbara, hat in hand, to say, "Barbara, you're not going to believe this, but I'm going to be at least three weeks (six months) late"? Isn't it the day I was due? Then, I'm going to be surprised and upset when the only way Barbara can manage is to bang her shoe on her desk. I've left her no time to take corrective action. I've left you with people waiting to work on something that isn't there. We're all in a crisis situation. We all look bad.

Let's back up three weeks. I know I'm slipping. Suppose I write my Weekly Status Report and tell Barbara: "I've hit trouble. Here's the problem, A—B—C. This is the action I'm taking to correct it, X—Y—Z. However, I still think we've got a potential three-week delay."

Now I've made it possible for Barbara to manage effectively. She can warn you, allowing your people to gear up for some interim assignment. Perhaps she can borrow someone from your unit to help me pick up the slack. After all, your people were planning to work on my material. They must know something about it. At the least, she can provide administrative support for my suggested solution. Whatever the outcome—even if the delay still occurs—we all look and function better.

I would also like to see data processors share solutions as well as problems. Many times, someone will come up with something that could be used to good advantage by others in the department. The person who developed this solution, however, is usually not in a position to know who else might use it. Only his management, aware of other activities and assignments in the area, can identify common applications and pass the good stuff along. None of us likes time-consuming, frustrating, and expensive duplication of effort. Unless information about things that work goes up, however, it rarely gets out.

4. Make personal evaluations.

We sometimes assume, because of verbal contact and day-to-day association, that our boss knows as much about what's going on as we do. We forget he or she is keeping track of more than our individual bailiwick. Management exposure to actual happenings in any one area of responsibility is generally fragmented. This makes it hard, if not impossible, for administrators to assess an event's overall impact without our assistance.

No one, your boss included, can know your job or the jobs of your people as well as you do. Only you can discern the effect of a problem or situation on work-in-progress. Even more important, only you can accurately gauge the effect of today's events on tomorrow's assignments. Let your Status Reports reflect your administrative judgment. When you abdicate your responsibility for personal evaluation, you belittle your own capabilities.

****

Keep in mind these techniques from SIX KEYS TO SUCCESS:

1. Be confident.

Writing a successful Status Report requires being confident with your material. You have to stay on top of what's going down in your sphere of responsibility.

Status reporting, however, also requires *self*-confidence. Each of us walks a thin line between what is legitimately our responsibility and those areas of concern that should be passed up the line. We all want to be "take charge" individuals. Yet, we know that lack of vital information can cripple administrative effectiveness. We recognize that an unaware management could ultimately cost us the autonomy we were trying to preserve.

Learn to feel confident with both your material and your approach in progress reporting. First, find out what is important to management in your department. Then, blend their requirements with your needs for administrative support and guidance. This puts you, and your Status Report, on solid ground.

2. Brevity and sequence.

Some data processors complain that their Status Reports are not carefully read. They insist that no one in management takes either current status or problem identification seriously. One reason for this lack of administrative concern in many organizations is overwriting. Readers who wade through bulky treatises on nothing once a week quickly become skeptical about any Status Report. Their attitude is, "You read one fairy tale and you've read them all."

Keep your Status Report brief when you can, and you'll establish a valuable precedent. If your reader then sees lots of prose on the page, he'll know you have something worthwhile to say.

Sequence is also a factor in gaining reader attention for our Status Reports. The familiar chronological sequence does not lead off with what is most important. To most management individuals, what's done is *done*.

A better approach is bad news first. Putting problem areas in the beginning immediately hits your reader with vital information. It's the existing and potential problems that will involve your management most directly.

One data processor complained to me that his boss never read far enough in a Status Report even to find out if there were problems. We corrected this situation easily by going to the bad-news-first sequence and using a creative heading. His next Status Report opened with the heading *Tragedy*. He got a careful and responsive reading.

3. Be specific.

This is particularly crucial, both in helping data processing management support corrective effort, and in improving our anticipation techniques.

For example, it would not have done any good for me to tell Barbara DiCocco, "I'm having trouble." In order to support or assist me, she must know what kind of trouble, action I plan to take, and the possible impact of the problem on my current task.

4. Explain your jargon.

This is included primarily for those of you who distribute copies of your Status Reports to your customers as well as to your management. Remember that the specialized terminology you use easily with your boss may "fog" readers outside your frame of reference.

One further caution. If your user does receive your Status Reports, there will be times when you will need to prepare two separate documents. In our Barbara DiCocco example, I certainly would not have forwarded a copy of my first Status Report to my customer. Since I gave Barbara time in which to act, she may be able to correct the situation. If she does, what would have been gained by panicking the user? Of course, if I found by next week's report that the slippage is still going to occur, I would copy the customer. He also deserves some advance notice.

****

Sample Status Report

The best way to evaluate your ability to produce a worthwhile Status Report is to role-play as if you were the recipient. Once you recognize what information would be critical to you as a manager, you should have a solid feel for the requirements of the administrative level above you.

Return for a moment to our continuing assignment for Mitchell. Assume I have been working on his request and I send the following Status Report to you, my immediate boss. It is prepared in the popular "headline" or "telegraph" style, with one or two brief sentences for each subject area.

Read each item carefully. Then, based on what I've told you, determine whether you know enough to manage effectively.

PHASE III COMPLETED ON TARGET 7/8, ACCEPTED 7/10
DOCUMENTATION SENT TO PROJECT CONTROL

KAREN ROBBINS AND GEORGE SHEEHAN DEVELOPED NEW PROCESSING METHOD

DELIVERY DELAYED ON THE DEDICATED PRINTER UNTIL 7/25

PHASE IV ETA MUST BE MOVED FROM 7/26 TO 8/24 DUE TO DELAY

PRODUCTION DATE MUST THEN MOVE FROM 9/1 TO 9/16

****

I'm sure you decided I did not provide enough information to allow you to meet your administrative responsibilities. For example:

1. Reader comprehension

What exactly took place in Phase III? If you employ Project Management or some other similar planning device, your Phases are probably the same for each assignment. In many shops, however, a phased approach is not used. In others, the number of Phases and their description vary, depending on the size and complexity of each job.

If either of these situations prevails in our hypothetical working environment, I should have pinpointed my Phase or Task III activity for you. After all, as a manager, you are keeping track of more than just my personal responsibilities.

"Phase III (Programming & Procedures Development—Systems Test) was completed . . . ."

This simple identification makes your job easier. You don't have to rely solely on memory or get out my original Phase or Task outline to bring yourself up to date.

Also, I told you Phase III was accepted. I did not specify by whom. Was it the customer? Was it Operations or the Systems Review (Quality Assurance) Committee? Where more than one acceptance requirement exists—and this is true in most organizations—I must note whose approval I received. In addition, I should inform you of my progress in obtaining the remaining necessary sign-offs.

2. New processing method

What is the new processing method, and why did I include it? If I was using praise as a motivational technique with my employees, I should have indicated that intention.

> "Karen Robbins and George Sheehan did an outstanding job in the development of a new processing method."

Furthermore, there should have been a "c:" notation followed by their names at the conclusion of my document. It won't do me any good to recognize their accomplishment if they don't know I've done so.

The new processing method could perhaps be useful elsewhere in our department. It might solve someone else's current problem or avoid costly duplication of effort. You, as the manager, are the only one who is fully aware of what other individuals and groups in our area are working on. You are the only one in a position to identify additional applications. You can't make such a judgment, however, unless you know what the new method actually does.

Now, I am not suggesting I include documentation of the new processing method with my Status Report. Yet, I could have briefly described its function or outlined its advantages—speeds up run time, for example. This would have provided sufficient information for you to decide if you should pursue the matter further.

3. Problem areas

I told you the delivery of the dedicated printer was delayed. Because of this, the Phase IV ETA will slip and the production date must be bumped. As you may know from personal experience, we can anticipate an inquiry from the user whenever a production date is moved. Mitchell is going to contact someone, and he is much more likely to call you—the person in charge—than me. Will you be able to answer his questions adequately?

Start with the printer. Why was it delayed? Was it my error or perhaps a truckers' strike? Mitchell is going to want to know, and I did not say. How great is the actual slippage? I only gave you one date—the new one. How can you gauge the amount of time lost unless I also tell you the original delivery date? Remember, we never give just one date—we always give *two*.

What about the current date of 7/25? Before you go on record, reinforcing that deadline for the user wouldn't you like to know its basis? I may have arrived at it simply out of wishful thinking. Maybe it represents a promise from the vendor's salesman. However the new date was determined—the truckers are going into binding arbitration on the 24th or whatever—I should have helped you evaluate its validity.

Now, consider Phase IV. Again, of course, I should have included a brief reminder of Phase IV's definition:

> "The ETA of Phase IV (System Acceptance & Closure) must be moved . . . ."

Your prime concern, however, and one of Mitchell's first questions is, "What have I explored as an alternative or interim solution?" Did I look into the possibility of Mitchell's borrowing time? Did I make any attempt whatsoever to prevent the Phase IV slippage and maintain the original production date? Even if I thoroughly explored every conceivable remedy and came up empty-handed, I should have documented my efforts.

Unless you can tell Mitchell exactly what I considered and why each was not workable, his conclusion has to be *we didn't try*. Only when you can confidently discuss alternatives (available or unavailable) is Mitchell reassured of our active concern.

How can you back me up—reaffirming your personal competency and that of our entire department—if you don't know what I've done?

4. Management anticipation

When I said the production date must move from 9/1 to 9/16, I also told you—by implication—that *I* will be tied up two additional weeks working on this assignment. Any people working for me are in the same bind.

You're a good manager. I can't believe you had nothing planned for me to start on 9/2. Read between the lines. Whatever subsequent assignment was on my schedule has to be at least two weeks late in getting started.

Go one step further. A good rule of thumb is to multiply by three. If I'm two weeks late beginning, I'll probably be six weeks late finishing. Several months down the road, I'm going to send you another Status Report with the repeat bombshell:

"Production date must then move from . . . to . . . ."

Heaven help us both if this next assignment is for the same user as the last one!

Doesn't it make sense to practice the management technique of anticipation *now?* How many data processing areas put out one brush fire after another, too caught up in solving one crisis to see it is already creating a future one?

Proper use of the Status Report can change this. I should have identified my next job and told you the effect my current slippage could have on its successful completion. At this point, armed with the assessment I provide, you would be in a good position to take some corrective action—realignment of dates or personnel, for example. Certainly, you'd have enough lead time to operate. At the least, difficulties I encounter in meeting my subsequent target will not come as an unpleasant surprise. You and I and the customer will be prepared.

****
Let's reorganize my initial Status Report to include the specific information you require.

SUBJECT: Product Liability Outstanding Loss System
DPSR # EX1992, PCN # 668
Status Report—July 7–July 11

PROBLEMS—
1. Truckers' strike has delayed delivery of the dedicated printer from 7/9 to 7/25, when truckers return to work under court order.

2. Without the printer, the ETA of Phase IV (System Acceptance and Closure) must move from 7/26 to 8/24.

3. This causes installation and scheduling conflicts, pushing the production date from 9/1 to 9/16. Mitchell has been informed.

4. Alternatives were explored, but no time-sharing is possible. (See attached memo and schedule from Operations.)

5. The two-week slippage will hold up initiation of Project XYZ from 9/2 until 9/17, leading me to anticipate the pushing of their target from 12/3 to 12/27.

COMPLETED ACTIVITY—
1. Phase III (Programming & Procedures Development—Systems Test) completed on target 7/8, accepted by customer 7/10.

2. Documentation sent to Project Control with approval requested by 7/14.

SPECIAL NOTES—
1. Karen Robbins and George Sheehan did an outstanding job in developing a new processing method that speeds run time by 30%. Documentation is available from George.

c: Karen Robbins
George Sheehan

The additional facts in this version allow more efficient utilization of the Status Report as a management tool. Equally important is the new sequence and the arrangement of the content under meaningful headings.

In Status Reports, as in any other document, bad news should come first. After all, problem situations are the most important aspect of status reporting from management's point of view. Activities completed are just that, *completed*. Special notes are interesting, but not vital. Immediate problems and any forecast we make available are what form the basis for effective administrative action.

15

The Phase Completion
Memo—Checkpoint

This document is called *Checkpoint* because it is written whenever we reach a milestone as outlined in our original Contract. As with our other communication vehicles, the actual names vary. In areas on a phased approach, it is the Phase Completion Memorandum or Report (other than the two Systems Contracts). In areas not on a phased approach, it is the Task Completion Memo. In operations, it becomes the Quarterly Report.

Customers love Checkpoint. They have complained for years that they never hear from DP unless there is a problem. Now, whatever you call it, this document brings the user into the mainstream of any data processing process at specified intervals. Problems or no problems, it allows him to monitor and evaluate progress step by step throughout any project or service. The communication channels are wide open.

Checkpoint also simplifies life for data processors. Rather than complaints or change requests at completion, we are now finding out about required modifications when they can be more easily handled. Necessary adjustments to the *what, when,* or *how much* are understood and authorized *as they surface* over the duration of our assignment.

Consider these elements:

1. State that the Phase, Task, or Quarter is complete. Present results, where appropriate.

Restate the goal for this Checkpoint as presented in the Contract. Tell the reader where you stand. If you have illustrative material that will help your user visualize progress to date, present it.

I am not suggesting offering anything as technically oriented as coding sheets to your customer. He wouldn't understand them and could hardly evaluate their effectiveness. We often, however, do have something—analytical results, completed schedules, suggested procedures, report format—that would assist our user in determining current status and future direction. These should be included.

2. Restate the original target date and costs. Give reasons for delays or cost overrun if they occurred.

Be sure your customer understands any deviations from the originally estimated time and cost at each Checkpoint. Provide exact amounts for both time slippage and increased expenditure. Also, document the reason(s) for such changes, both for your future reference and to clarify cause as well as effect for your user.

3. Ask for adjustment of time schedule or costs if necessary.

Problems encountered in one Phase, Task, or Quarter can impact remaining estimates. Now is the time to request any needed adjustments to time and cost in the next item on our Contract schedule.

All too frequently, we have waited until project or service completion to inform our user of overall changes to originally projected time and cost. This procrastination meant the amounts were large and justification was difficult. By explaining required changes as they occur, we can hit the customer with smaller and more easily explained increases.

4. Discuss any outstanding or foreseeable problem areas.

This is a necessary exercise at each Checkpoint. We all know it is impossible to anticipate all contingencies at the initiation of any data processing activity. Once we are engaged in the requested project or service, we are better able to identify areas of potential concern. Use this document to alert and involve your user.

5. Restate the next Phase, Task, or Quarter objectives, time schedule, and estimated cost.

Our customers have this information available in their copy of our Contract. Remember, however, that we may be asking for a modification to the original at this Checkpoint. If so, spell it out.

Even if there are no changes, restate the initial projections. Many users do not retrieve their copy of the Contract, relying on a sometimes faulty memory to reassess future goals. Also, we may be coming up on a Phase, Task, or Quarter in which the customer's commitment will be called due. Use your brief restatement to jog his memory.

6. Ask for approval of the completed Phase, Task, or Quarter and authorization to proceed to the next.

As with the Contract, Checkpoint documents must be signed. In fact, unless we obtain written approval for what we've done and anything that's changed, we could invalidate our Contract.

Consider what we are asking our user to approve. His sign-off verifies his agreement with results, time usage, and cost to date—*whether or not* they remain as originally stated in the Contract. His signature also gives us the go-ahead for the *what, when,* and *how much* of the next Phase, Task, or Quarter—either as initially presented or *as modified* at this Checkpoint.

Again, as with the Contract, two copies can be prepared and forwarded to the customer. If he has no questions or suggested modifications, he simply signs one copy and returns it to DP.

7. Maintain a proper distribution list.

Checkpoint documents keep everyone involved with a project or service up-to-date. Not only do they report current status, they announce any changes to originally established goals, time schedule, and cost.

Be sure anyone who received a copy of the initial Contract receives all Checkpoint correspondence. Also, add to the copy list any individuals or groups mentioned for the first time in the Checkpoint document you are currently distributing.

****

Review these techniques from SIX KEYS TO SUCCESS prior to writing Checkpoint:

1. Get your objectives firmly in mind.

Checkpoint has more potential objectives than any other communication vehicle in the DP life cycle. It is easily adapted to numerous essential applications—both work-oriented and administrative. Creative data processors in any organization can take advantage of its unlimited flexibility.

Here are the five usages I encounter most frequently:

A. Direct involvement of the user. Many customers feel only minimally involved in *their* project or service. Now, however, Checkpoint places them directly and continuously in the center of the action. This is an invaluable educational function. By expecting our customers to participate directly in decision-making or problem-solving activities, we give them a sense of ownership. Ownership produces responsibility. In most instances, a cooperative rapport is established. Mutual effort is encouraged.

B. Step-by-step commitment and approval. This function works greatly to our advantage. We are now able to isolate and correct any customer dissatisfaction as we proceed. Each user can see what he is (and is not) getting step by step. Changes are simplified because they can be made prior to end result.

For example, necessary adjustments to systems specifications can be brought to our attention by the user early in the development process. Certainly, this is preferable to frustrating and expensive modification in a production environment.

We also now have *written* approval for all that takes place over the duration of a project or service. We know our customers have read and understood what's going on. If they hadn't, they wouldn't commit themselves by signing. No one can come back to us at completion and say we overlooked or ignored user requirements. Those signatures clear our actions at every stage.

C. Improved estimating. I'm sure all of us would agree that adequate estimating of time and cost is a nationwide problem. Few organizations have anywhere near the accuracy record they would like.

A major factor in our failure to correct our estimating has been the difficulty in pinpointing *exactly where* we started to go wrong on previous assignments. Unfortunately, this is particularly true when a project or service has been lengthy in duration. We tend to concentrate on the largest amount of time slippage and cost overrun, which usually occurs toward completion. This limits our focus to our final Phase or Task. The actual problem, however, probably began early in our activities and simply snowballed. Hindsight rarely uncovers this problem's *source*. Checkpoint does.

Corporations now using Checkpoint as an internal administrative tool are seeing their estimates improve by as much as 80%. They wait until they have Checkpoint documents for a number of assignments. Then, they look through all of them to determine where slippage first began in each. Not surprisingly, most are finding that their difficulties consistently begin in the *same* Phase or Task. Also, they now not only know *where* things went awry, they know *why*. (See above, element 2.)

For example, development areas using a phased approach found their slippage beginning most frequently in two Phases—Programming and Systems Test. Of course, the reasons for the problems varied. One group discovered their programmers were working from lousy résumés, meaning their problem was actually the Detail Design Phase. Another determined that their programmers lacked training and experience equal to the type of work being requested.

Whatever the actual cause, each unit could now take specific steps to correct the situation and improve their estimates on subsequent projects. At the least, they knew to increase future time and cost estimates for the problem phases until solutions could be implemented.

D. Documentation. Few of us enjoy doing Systems Documentation. Too often, because of time constraints, we wind up attempting to document even large-scale systems mainly by hindsight. The job is difficult, and the end result is rarely as useful a tool as it should be.

Make it easy on yourself. Where Checkpoint documents are written properly, with appropriate illustrative material, documentation is done logically and effectively—step by step. No extra writing. No tedious reconstruction of months of effort. Everything required, including user involvement, is noted. The entire documentation package is sitting right in front of you at System Closure.

E. Corporate requirements for System Review or Quality Assurance. There is no need to spend valuable time preparing a separate report for the Systems Review Board or Quality Assurance Committee in your organization. Simply copy them with your Checkpoint document.

In fact, overall evaluation of new systems and services is much faster and more accurate with Checkpoint. Members of the review groups stay on top of your established or changing objectives. Also, having monitored the entire activity through step-by-step information, they can act quickly to approve end result.

2. Have all materials at hand.

Checkpoint only works when all appropriate material is readily available. Unless pertinent information is carefully retained, you could reach the completion of a lengthy Phase or Task only to find you must create a Checkpoint document from memory.

If your organization employs the team concept, one team member should be designated as scribe. He then maintains an up-to-date working or Checkpoint file. If you are autonomous in your responsibilities, the job is yours. Don't come up on Checkpoint empty-handed.

3. Explain your jargon.

This will become less and less of a consideration as you move through your Checkpoints. The definitions presented in past documents should enable your readers to follow you more easily in the present one.

Do not forget, however, that other departments and management groups may be receiving "informational" copies. If you have any reservations at all about reader comprehension, I again suggest including a brief glossary.

4. Maintain a two-way channel of communication.

With this document, we are looking for feedback from our user and other readers.

In order to use such feedback effectively, we must start building *communication time* into our original estimates.

The average turn-around for Checkpoint is four working days. This increases, of course, if the user responds with questions, or a Review Committee situation is involved. If you are still basing your initial estimates on lapsed time—backing start dates up against stop dates—you will be late from the beginning with Checkpoint.

Estimate with specific time framework, looking at a calendar. You certainly don't want your four communication days to fall over Labor Day weekend. Give your customer time to evaluate, comment on, and approve your results at each Checkpoint. Meaningful dialogue is never hurried.

Should you be running late on the completion of a Task or Phase, however, don't let your turn-around time make you even later. Where your user is in the same geographic location, hand-carry your Checkpoint document, discuss it, and obtain user approval.

The one approach I don't like is the "If I don't hear from you by September 4, I will assume you agree" tag line. This can only be used successfully when the writer retains final option. In most organizations, the user could still come back after September 4 with modifications or a flat no. Where does that leave a data processor who has already allocated personnel or other resources to a now changed or completely defunct objective?

$$* *$$

Sample Phase Completion Memo—Checkpoint

Once again, try preparing your own document. Let's assume you have been working on Mitchell's system. You've concluded Phase III as specified in the Contract and are ready to present the following in a Checkpoint Memorandum or Report.

PHASE III COMPLETED JULY 8 AT A COST OF $2,050.00 (20.5 PERSON DAYS).

ORIGINALLY ESTIMATED COMPLETION—JULY 8 AT COST OF $1,980.00 (19.8 PERSON DAYS).

SAMPLE OUTPUT LISTING NOT AVAILABLE UNTIL JUNE 29, CAUSING MISSED DEADLINE AND COST OVERRUN.

ADDITIONAL PERSONNEL ASSIGNED TO MEET ORIGINAL PHASE IV ETA OF JULY 26.

WILL START PHASE IV ON JULY 11.

In most data processing shops, if we came this close to our initial estimate, what would we say? Hooray—we made it—the beer's on me! I deliberately made this example ridiculously close to show that in order for Checkpoint to work, you must document *any* deviation from the Systems Contract, however small. Here are three important reasons:

One, if you do not record all deviation of any size, you—in effect—negate the Systems Contract. Phase Completion or Checkpoint is an amendment to the Contract and must be accurate.

Two, we all know that small slippage in one Phase, Task, or Quarter can effect large slippage in a subsequent one. The Checkpoint cannot be used as an internal administrative tool for improving estimates if we do not document when slippage—no matter how minor—*first* began.

Three, if we do not take small amounts of slippage or cost overrun seriously, we have no credibility with our customer when we must go to him with large deviations. Only when we demonstrate concern over smaller variations will users acknowledge our good intentions in a crisis situation.

Also, examine the cause of your difficulty in Phase III. In our sample situation, who was supposed to provide the initial output listing format? Wasn't it the user? Here, failure of our customer to meet his commitment has resulted in lost time and increased cost. Isn't this often the case? With Checkpoint, you must document such responsibility for two reasons:

One, once the customer recognizes that meeting his commitments is crucial, he should improve his department's participation in subsequent Phases, Tasks, or Quarters.

Two, again, in order to use Checkpoint to upgrade our own performance on subsequent assignments, we must record not only when slippage first began, but *why*.

* *

Now, evaluate your completed Checkpoint carefully.

1. Reader comprehension

Did you ensure that your reader understood exactly what was accomplished in Phase III? Did you provide for illustrative material to graphically depict positive result? We cannot rely on any reader to get out a copy of the original Contract and review the specified objectives. Completion is meaningless unless each reader understands *what* was completed.

It also helps if you do the arithmetic for your respondent. A slippage of .7 person days and a cost overrun of $70 is immediately comprehensible. When you present $2,050.00 (20.5) and $1,980.00 (19.8), your reader instinctively stops reading and begins mentally subtracting. You've lost his full attention.

2. Reason for time slippage and cost overrun

This is not a good time to get into a "finger-pointing" situation. If you took the approach, "John Jones from your area blew it"—you are asking for a similar or worse response from the customer should you ever be in error. A simple declarative sentence stating what occurred is sufficient.

Remember, however, we never present just one date. Help your reader gauge the impact of nonperformance by including the date the output listing was expected as well as the day it actually was received.

3. Changes to Phase IV

Did you provide adequate detail concerning the additional personnel necessary to maintain the integrity of the original Phase IV date? "Additional personnel" alone is a meaningless generality. The reader must understand how many people, their level (or title), and any increased cost they may represent. Detailing the number of people shows you've done your homework. Explaining level or function helps the reader understand what these people will be doing—why they are needed. Certainly, any reader seeing additional people thinks cost and will expect to know exact amount. Even if you are pulling the old "more people, same amount of person days" routine with no increased cost, say so. Otherwise, you will get a phone call instead of a sign-off.

4. Salesmanship

You have made the professional decision that it is crucial to maintain the original Phase IV ETA. Your reader, however, could elect not to accept the necessary additional people and their cost. He may say: "Just let the Phase IV date slip. I don't want to pay the extra tab." Only by explaining the consequences of this alternative can you convince the reader that your decision represents good judgment.

Did you tell the reader how much the Phase IV date would slip without the additional personnel? Did you spell out the cost such slippage could trigger? Further, if the Phase IV date goes, subsequent target dates—including the production date—surely will be jeopardized. Show a reader such end results and your appropriate preventive action looks highly acceptable.

. Please note that any consequences must be presented in the reader's frame of reference. Tell Mitchell you need to maintain the Phase IV date in order to facilitate your other assignments, and he is not likely to be overly concerned.

One caution. We only slipped perhaps one day in Phase III. If the possible slippage in Phase IV were to be much greater than that—say, two weeks—always explain why. We understand how a one-day slippage in one Phase can create larger amounts of slippage later. We've all encountered the problems of vacation schedules, unavailability of testing facilities, etc. Our customers do not always make the connection.

5. Approval and authorization

It's tempting in this document to link these two together, asking for them jointly as our tag line.

"Please let me have your approval for Phase III and authorization to begin Phase IV by (date)."

This approach is not always effective, particularly in a case like this where we are changing something about Phase IV.

For example, if I offer you a total package and you don't like one part of it—what is your reaction to the entire presentation? Isn't it negative? This is why unpopular amendments are tacked onto legislative bills. The entire bill is often vetoed to get rid of one amendment, throwing the baby out with the bath water.

In this instance, you need Phase III out of the way. At the least, you want Mitchell to cross it off mentally before he considers your Phase IV proposal. We discussed techniques that allow a reader to shift gears mentally between topics. Such an approach would be valuable here.

Did you consider dividing your Checkpoint document into two separate sections under appropriate headings? This would encourage your reader to finish his review of Phase III, avoiding any linkage between it and possible disagreement with your changes to Phase IV. Certainly, any negotiation regarding your decision to assign additional personnel to Phase IV should not postpone acceptance of your work effort in Phase III.

* *

Here is a possible sequence for the Phase III Completion Memo. It allows for easy reader understanding and acceptance, while meeting the requirements of our other usage of this document.

SUBJECT: Product Liability Outstanding Losses
DPSR# EX1992, PCN# 668
Phase III Completion

PHASE III—Description exactly as presented in the Contract with commitments, estimated dates, and estimated costs (See enclosed results)

1. We encountered a time slippage of .7 person days and a cost overrun of $70.

2. This occurred because the sample output listing expected (date) was not received until June 29.

3. Please review results and forward approval of Phase III by (date).

PHASE IV—Description exactly as presented in the Contract with commitments, estimated dates, and estimated costs

1. (assignment of personnel) I have assigned 2 additional Systems Analysts at a cost of (amount) to assure the original Phase IV Completion date. They are needed to . . . .

2. (consequences) If we do not assign these people, the Phase IV date will slip 2 weeks as we will lose access to testing facilities. This delay could cost an additional (amount). Slippage on Phase IV could also push the Production Date 2 weeks, again increasing implementation costs by (amount).

3. Please let me have your authorization to begin Phase IV, as amended, by July 10 so that we may begin on schedule July 11.

4. Thank you.

Signed copies: Manager, DP area or company
                 Manager, customer area or company

Informational copies: Anyone who received a copy of the original Contract.
                      Additional personnel to be assigned to Phase IV.

* *

In assessing the effectiveness of this sequence, begin with the Subject heading. The name of the project or service and the associated numbers, of course, are still important. The phrase ''Completion of Phase III'' makes usage easier for anyone employing Checkpoint as a documentation or administrative tool at a later date. Instead of reading full page after page, he need only read the Subject heading of each to retrieve the document he wants.

We also have eliminated a sentence from the context of our Memorandum. We do not have to open with, ''Phase III was completed . . . .'' The reader knows immediately he has a Completion Report.

The content and phrasing of the Topic headings dividing our Checkpoint into two sections will greatly increase reader understanding. By repeating the exact description of Phase III from the Contract, we remind our reader—with minimum prose—of the Phase III objectives. Restatement of Phase III also makes it unnecessary to press user responsibility for the delayed output listing. His commitment is clearly spelled out in the original Contract definition. Further, we now do not have to repeat initial time and cost estimates in our discussion of slippage and cost overrun. They also are an integral part of the Phase III specifications.

Reviewing such a Topic heading brings the reader immediately back into the picture. It re-creates an accurate perception of the originally projected Phase III work flow, preparing the reader for valid consideration of end result.

If material illustrating specific achievement is available, this Topic heading also facilitates good use of ''interruption'' techniques. Immediately following the Phase III description, we ''interrupt'' with ''(See enclosed results).'' The reader can then inspect actual work completed—comparing it with the forecasted objectives—before moving on to further discussion.

The Phase IV Contract description is also an excellent Topic heading. It jogs the reader's memory as to where we now proceed, including any commitment of his that may be called due. When changes are necessary and consequences must be outlined—as in our sample—this restatement often provides excellent incentive for acceptance of suggested adjustments. The reader instantly sees the direct contrast between projected future accomplishment, as defined in the heading, and the catastrophes that could result when DP recommendations are rejected.

By asking for approval immediately at the conclusion of our Phase III section, we encourage our reader to think of Phase III as *past tense*. Requesting authorization to proceed with Phase IV *separately,* directly following the presentation of necessary changes, should keep any negotiation the reader feels is required strictly related to Phase IV.

Of course, if there are no problems in one Phase and no proposed changes to the subsequent Phase, the sign-off procedure can be simplified. With everything remaining as originally agreed upon in the Contract, you can add signature lines to your Checkpoint document. DP then signs one, and both are forwarded to the customer. Remember, however, still to ask for the return of a user-signed copy by a specific date. This is best done by re-emphasizing the start date for the next Phase or Task and your need for a response prior to that date.

16

Department Highlights

We discussed the role of the Status Report in vertical communication upward through administrative levels in a data processing department. Department Highlights provide vertical dissemination of information back down from the top and horizontally to other concerned administrators.

The time span for distribution of this "report from management" varies from organization to organization or even from department to department. Most familiar is a *Monthly* Department Highlights, but such documents are also prepared weekly or quarterly—depending on need and the size of the shop involved.

Department Highlights are greatly dependent on (Weekly) Status Reports for content. In addition to administrative or corporate announcements, they present an interpretative synopsis of accomplishments and problems compiled from internal Status Reports. Of course, all such material is evaluated, usually by the department manager, for relevance and general interest. Overall significance and potential impact on the department are also important considerations.

Not all organizations write Department Highlights, and it's too bad. Just as we noted the DP manager's difficulty in operating in a void, data processing employees find it frustrating to always be the last to know critical administrative decisions and actions. Turning out the jobs, maintaining good morale—everything is easier when Department Highlights provide across-the-board access to pertinent departmental status and future outlook.

Some or all of these elements may be included in Department Highlights based on available information:

1. Outline current status by project or job. Include Phase or Task completion, anticipated time schedules, and costs.

This information is especially useful where different Phases or Tasks of the same assignment are the responsibility of separate units within a department. Any group waiting for results or freed-up manpower should know if delays occur or if work is moving faster than expected.

Such presentation of progress to date also affords an overview of current departmental status. Supervisors, team or shift leaders, and other administrators can use this in the determining and updating of personnel allocation and vacation schedules.

Do not be afraid that such distribution of status will cause bad feeling on the part of those who are late or over cost. As long as Department Highlights are not used as an ax by DP management, the competition that develops is normal and healthy. Such open posting of results can even be an incentive to greater productivity. Also, those projects and jobs encountering difficulties often get an assist from others in the department. People can only volunteer help when they know there's a problem.

2. Forecast objectives by job or project for the next reporting period.

This notifies individuals within the department who are waiting for results or people of *anticipated* Phase or Task completion. Where target dates have not changed, they are secure in maintaining their already established objectives. If the time framework has altered, they have time to adequately adjust their schedules.

Departments with a heavy work load find such forecasting also encourages good time management by everyone—from manager to trainee. Instead of going off in all directions at once, employees plan their daily activity according to departmental priorities and the *current* time constraints for each.

3. Share solutions.

This document is an excellent vehicle for presenting good news. Anything occurring in one area of the department that could benefit other individuals or units should be discussed. Subjects vary depending on department responsibilities—development of a new form or more efficient processing method, changed or additional usage of software, improved administrative procedures, etc.

Of course, extensive detail cannot be effectively included in Department Highlights. If the suggestion or solution is complex or lengthy, provide a brief summary and supply the name of the individual to be contacted for further information. Anyone seeing an application for the solution in his unit can then contact that person for the specifics.

4. Discuss personnel.

Department Highlights allow any management to employ praise as a motivational

technique. Promotions, performance bonus awards, and other warranted appreciation should be announced. This not only acknowledges and reinforces existing
good performance, but it motivates other employees to strive for such recognition.

Congratulations may be extended for accomplishment that is not work-
related—election to public office, volunteer service in the community, marriage,
the birth of a child. Such personalization within a department builds a sense of
community or "team" orientation and strengthens all internal working relationships. (See "Congratulate where appropriate," page 48.)

Department Highlights are also suitable vehicles for the discussion of personnal
allocation and need. Changing personnel assignments are of interest to everyone in
a department. Keeping employees informed as to who is involved in or responsible
for any given job ensures direct channels of communication between people and
working units.

Need for additional personnel, both numbers and classification, should be
noted. Other administrators may have people available or know where specific
types of talent can be obtained. Employees within the department—if they are not
interested in the new job themselves—may have friends with just the right
qualifications and experience. Department Highlights help tap all internal sources
and may greatly simplify any necessary recruitment.

5. Mention training opportunities.

Bring the entire department up-to-date on any new or revised training programs
available in your organization or department. The fact that education is mentioned
at all is a tacit endorsement by management of each employee's attempting to
improve his or her personal skills.

Also useful is a brief critique of any class attended by department employees
during the reporting period. The comments of actual participants on seminar
content, structure, and applicability are the best possible guide to other employees
considering similar training.

Certainly, if a particular program is well taught and highly pertinent to current
assignments, Department Highlights should spread the word. Others in the department will now know its value and be encouraged to attend. If, on the other
hand, a class is a bomb, such information should be distributed before other
employees waste work time to attend it.

6. Consider customer relationships, where appropriate.

Present a concise description of current customer orientation. Include specific
expectations, examples of the benefits of mutual cooperation, and, perhaps, areas
of disagreement. This prevents anyone from your department from going into a

user "cold" and possibly making an already difficult situation worse. Particularly helpful is a breakdown of communication with the customer—agreements reached or a report on negotiations in progress.

This section of Department Highlights may also be used to forecast probable future user need. Your analysis of forthcoming customer requirements may be based on discussion with user areas or other factors, such as announced changes to State and Federal Regulations. Planned expansion of a particular application or a necessary system update are also good indicators. Outlining such potential assignments, even when they are not yet firm, invites suggestions and comments early and facilitates better management planning.

7. Detail arrangements with supporting departments or outside consultants.

Let everyone know the involvement of outside groups in any departmental activity. This is especially important to acceptance by employees of any outside consultant(s) working in your department.

Be equally specific about arrangements with other groups within your own organization. List requests for forms design, printing, source data, hardware, procedures, simulation, testing, whatever. Having access to such information reinforces departmental timetables for those employees involved. It also avoids having every unit in your department hit a support group—like testing—at the same time. Everyone can plan around peak periods of activity in the support areas, ensuring easier access to necessary service.

* *

Remember these techniques from SIX KEYS TO SUCCESS if preparing Department Highlights is your responsibility:

1. Present facts.

Only accurate and honest information is acceptable in this document. Hedging or "sins of omission" quickly disillusion department employees. Rumors flourish because everyone is skeptical of management's "story."

If you don't know all the facts or are not in a position to publish them, *say so* and table the topic until you can be straight with your readers. No one is going to use Department Highlights as an information source or a planning and evaluation tool unless he can trust its content.

2. Logical flow to ideas and paragraphs.

Since readers of Department Highlights may not be *directly* involved in the topics discussed, arrange your content to assist reader comprehension. This document is easiest to use when it follows chronological sequence within each main heading. The headings themselves should be arranged in order of importance, allowing any reader easy access to his primary interests. Most writers begin with CURRENT DEPARTMENT STATUS and work through to PERSONNEL BULLETINS. However, what is most important to readers of any Department Highlights—and therefore the best sequence—must be determined by the writer. Each department's priorities will be different.

3. Brevity.

As with (Weekly) Status Reports, Department Highlights can be overdone. If you don't have anything to say, follow this simple procedure:

One, be sure to include accustomed headings anyway.

Two, place a brief comment like "nothing new" under any heading where material is not available.

This tells your readers you *did look* for announcements or comment pertinent to each segment. They do not have to ask you, "What about . . . ?" You also will have a more interested and enthusiastic audience for what you do say. You haven't worn out anyone's patience by writing a great deal about nothing.

4. Always personalize.

This is an internal document. Most of the readers know each other or, at least, know of each other. This makes it easy to use people's names, recognizing individual effort and developing a "colleague" atmosphere. Knowing "who" as well as "what" makes each employee more comfortable with the interpersonal relationships necessary in his environment.

One caution. Department Highlights is *not* a vehicle for condemnation or even reasonable criticism. Blame may fall on an individual simply because he is noted as being responsible for a particular job that went wrong. The "finger pointing," however, is *only* by implication and never direct statement. Taking someone to task, in writing and before the entire department, can only put that individual on the defensive. It also creates fear and hostility among other employees. Their question has to be, "Who's next?"

5. Be careful with distribution.

Each department must determine its own Highlights distribution list, and need-to-know is the primary criterion. Information in the Highlights document is intended for use only by people *inside* a department or group. Such individuals, because of close association, understand what's said and how to use it. When distribution goes too far *outside* the department's limits, readers are unfamiliar with topics, names, and intentions. They easily misunderstand content and misinterpret department attitudes, creating problems for everyone involved.

* *

Sample Department Highlights

Let's assume Monthly Department Highlights are distributed in our area. Try writing only that section of the Highlights document pertaining to Mitchell's project. (All other current projects in the department would be discussed also, but we do not need to concern ourselves with them in the sample.)
Incorporate the following information:

PROJECT BEHIND SCHEDULE.

ESTIMATED PHASE III ETA WAS JULY 7—COMPLETED JULY 8— WITH SLIPPAGE OF .7 PERSON DAYS.

SAMPLE OUTPUT LISTING EXPECTED JUNE 6 NOT RECEIVED UNTIL JUNE 29.

SUE NOLTON AND DAN REDFIELD ASSIGNED TO PHASE IV TO MAINTAIN ORIGINAL ETA OF JULY 26.

THEY WILL ASSIST IN PREPARATION OF CLOSURE DOCUMENTS.

PHASE IV TO BEGIN JULY 11.

DELAY APPROVED BY MITCHELL AND ACTUARIAL DP COMMITTEE.

DEDICATED PRINTER TO BE DELIVERED JULY 25.

MARTHA MURPHY IN FORMS DEVELOPMENT UNIT SENT THE FINAL DRAFT OF THE OUTPUT FORMAT TO PRINTING SERVICES.

DELIVERY OF OUTPUT FORMS TO OPERATIONS SCHEDULED FOR JULY 14.

BARBARA DICOCCO PROMOTED TO MANAGER, SYSTEMS DEVELOPMENT.

* *

Review your completed material as if you were in our department, but not directly involved with the Product Liability Outstanding Loss project. Would you understand current status and personnel and support group utilization, as well as future objectives?

1. Reader comprehension

Where more than one assignment is discussed in the same communication vehicle, each must be separated from the others and fully identified. In Department

Highlights, the easiest way to ensure instant reader recognition of content is the use of headings—usually the system or service name and numbers.

Not only will the reader understand exactly what is being discussed, but he can turn immediately to those sections of the Highlights most closely related to his interests. Certainly, any reader wants to review the material that could impact his job responsibilities *first*. He can then scan the remainder of the Highlights, keeping up-to-date with overall area work-flow and any announcements.

As in the Checkpoint document and the Status Report, it is important in Department Highlights to define any Phases or Tasks referenced. Others in our department may not be sure of the specific activity taking place in Phase III or scheduled for Phase IV.

Also, again as in the Checkpoint, you should have included an objective statement of user responsibility for the delayed sample output listing. There may be others in our department who either are working with or will be working with Mitchell's area. Your explanation of the delay—without any finger pointing—subtly alerts them to the possibility of similar difficulties in their dealings with this customer.

2. Cost

Most organizations employing the Department Highlights vehicle are most specific about dates and any time slippage. Far too many, however, still ignore the crucial element of *cost*. Did you include it?

We've discussed the increasing nationwide concern with—if not insistence upon—adequate DP cost accounting. One of the best ways to start each member of a department thinking in terms of actual dollars spent is to present costing figures in your Highlights. Two reasons:

One, the wide internal circulation of this document ensures that cost becomes an accepted criterion in any work evaluation.

Two, individual awareness that management does consider cost important is a giant step toward better overall control. More careful initial estimating becomes the norm. Overruns are taken more seriously. After all, any employee who knows his original figures and deviations from them will be published among his peers quickly becomes intensely cost-conscious.

3. Utilization of supporting departments

I'm sure you mentioned that Martha Murphy from our forms development unit had sent the necessary output format to Printing Services. You probably also stated that the printed forms were scheduled for delivery to Operations July 14.

This is vital information for anyone else in our department planning to utilize Printing Services in the near future. At the least, he or she knows Printing has already allocated time to us and may be reluctant to accept additional requests—particularly if they are large or complex.

We still don't have all the necessary information, however. Did you remember to include the date on which Martha submitted the format? Without that date, no one in our department can gauge the turn-around time Martha is experiencing.

If I were coming up on a Task requiring printing support, it would help me to know Printing Services' current workload. Martha's timetable is an excellent clue. If I know her time framework, I can either decide to proceed as I planned or begin to readjust my schedule, anticipating a possible printing delay.

Always, please, give *two* dates—not one.

4. Rumors and speculation

Barbara DiCocco has been promoted to Manager of Systems Development. If you worked in the same department with Barbara, wouldn't that news prompt some mental questions? Questions like, "Is she going to keep the same staff?"—"Who is she replacing (if anyone) and where is that person going?"—"Who's in line for her old job?"—etc.

Incomplete information is a prime source of unfounded rumors and uneasy speculation, both of which waste working hours in nonproductive employee conversation and can severely damage employee morale.

Full disclosure of what is known, as well as what remains to be decided, eliminates a good portion of these problems. Why not use the Department Highlights as your forum?

Take Barbara's promotion. Be sure everyone knows the date on which it became (becomes) effective. If she is replacing someone, that individual should be named. Try also to include the preceding manager's fate, if you know it—promoted (to what position?), transferred (to what department?), or left the company (going where?).

If Barbara's former position has been filled, say so and by whom. If it has not, state that the decision is pending. Above all, if her old job has been eliminated or organizational structure does not require a replacement, make this clear. Otherwise, you are sure to have at least some employees secretly competing for a nonexistent promotion.

In some instances, where the promotion announced is to a significant or policy-making level, you might present some direct comment—say, from Barbara herself—on future plans. Nothing quells half-truths and unnecessary worry about administrative realignment faster than straight talk from the horse's mouth (with all due apologies to Barbara).

Above all, in announcing a step up for anyone, be congratulatory. Did you just include the flat statement that Barbara had been promoted, or did you extend a "pat-on-the-back" from the entire department?

Remember, recognition of accomplishment in any Department Highlights should motivate every other employee to a higher standard of personal performance.

* *

Here is an outline of our section of the Department Highlights that affords an accurate assessment of current area activity. Reader questions are anticipated and fully answered. Note, also, that the sequence moves the reader(s) easily from accomplished fact through projected goals to items of general interest.

Product Liability Outstanding Losses

DPSR# EX1992, PCN# 668

CURRENT STATUS—

1. Phase III (Programming & Procedures Development—Systems Test) due July 7, finished July 8 with a slippage of .7 person days and a cost overrun of $70.

2. (why) The sample output listing expected from Actuarial June 6 was received June 29.

3. Martha Murphy (forms development unit) forwarded final draft of the output format to Printing Services on July 9.

4. The delay and cost overrun have been approved by Mark Mitchell and the Actuarial DP Committee.

FUTURE OBJECTIVES—

1. Phase IV (System Acceptance & Closure) will begin July 11.

2. Sue Nolton and Dan Redfield have been assigned to Phase IV to maintain the original ETA of July 26.

3. (why) They will assist in the preparation of the necessary Closure documents.

4. Printing Services will deliver the output forms to Operations on July 14.

5. The dedicated printer needed for the first production run will be delivered July 25.

ANNOUNCEMENTS—

1. Congratulations are in order to Barbara DiCocco, former Project Co-ordinator, who was promoted to Manager of Systems Development on July 9.

2. Barbara is replacing Stan Johnson, who left the corporation to join a firm in Arizona.

3. Congratulations also to Denis Jacques, who will assume Barbara's prior duties as Project Co-ordinator when Phase IV begins on July 11.

c: Internal Distribution List (determined by each department).
Any individual mentioned by name who is not normally on distribution.
Printing Services.

17

Project or Service Completion Memo—The Closure

This document is written when we have attained the end result as specified in our Contract. In a development area on a phased approach, it is the Phase Completion Report for either Phase I V or Phase VI, depending on the total number of phases. Where Task definition or some other planning device is employed, it becomes the Project Closure. In data processing areas not engaged in systems development, such as methods and procedures, it is a Service Closure. In an operations context, most organizations call it the Year-end Report and it is distributed to close-out annual Service Contracts.

Data processing needs a Closure device. We have discussed the nationwide problem of inaccurate time and cost estimates and inadequate cost-justification methods. Certainly, a primary reason for our poor track record is the fact that in many DP environments *nothing is ever finished*. Projects and services tend to remain open-ended, with constant modification, enhancement, and change the order of the day. How can we ever correctly estimate anything if there is never a cut-off?

Part of our difficulty is semantics. Part is our way of doing business. Both can be changed through more effective communication.

Take semantics. Perhaps the best example of differing data processing and user expectations in a development effort is the word "operational." As a data processor, how do you define it? Most of us would say: "It's working (thank God)—it runs." Consider the customer, however. How does he or she define "operational"? Users I've questioned say: "It does everything I want, better than I thought it would. It's scheduled when I need it run. My people know how to correctly input the system. They know how to utilize the output. All the associated procedures are functioning easily and efficiently."

There are few, if any "operational" systems by any customer's definition.

Another often misunderstood word is "maintenance." DP is firm on this one. We proclaim maintenance as corrective or additional work necessary *to maintain* a system. Then, we struggle day to day with the user's definition of "maintenance"—*on-going development.*

What about our traditional way of doing business? In many organizations, the scenario would go something like this.

I am your customer, Martha Mitchell. I get my first report, look at it, and call you. "Hi," I say pleasantly. "I just got my Product Liability Outstanding Loss listing and I was thinking. It's inconvenient to have the date on the right-hand side. Why don't we move it to the left?"

You say some bad words under your breath, then smile into the telephone. "No problem, Martha. You want the date on the left-hand side, we'll put the date on the left-hand side." (We can do anything.)

Now, however, you have to pull people off other jobs to do it. It might take one day. It might take three. What's happening to the time and cost estimates for the work that must stand still while you move my date?

Later, I call you again. "Hey," I begin, "the date looks great, but my boss would really like 50 lines on the page, not 52. He can't read the last two lines that well. He wears glasses."

"OK, Martha, OK," you respond. It's a *simple* job, right? You just assign someone to get in and get out. Unfortunately—and this happens frequently—going in to futz around changing the number of lines on the page seems to create other internal problems. Your *simple* adjustment generates a raft of programming complications. Bugs appear that just weren't there before. They have to be resolved. Do we ever know how much time or how much money is actually eaten up by this kind of situation?

The only cure to such frustrating and disorganized work-flow is to firmly establish the communication cycle we've been considering. Where necessary communication vehicles are prepared and distributed—Initiation to *Closure*—such confusion and waste cannot occur.

Here are the important Closure elements:

1. State that the project or service is complete according to the original specifications.

For the first time, we are in a position to go to our user and say, "It's over." Why can we do this now, when we have often been unable to do so in the past?

One, we have a signed Contract. In it, the user agreed, in writing, to the end result we have now provided.

Two, we have Checkpoint. We have sign-offs step by step, not only for everything we've done, but anything that changed.

2. Ask for customer approval.

The user signs. Generally, this is not a problem. He has already reviewed and approved all actions over the duration of the project or service. There should be few surprises at this stage.

Be firm about a sign-off where necessary, however, or this assignment could hang around the rest of your professional life. One customer I knew did refuse to sign the Closure for his system. The manager of the DP development department was polite, but firm. "Take all the time you require," he replied. "Review all test results. Check with your people. This system does *not* go into production or Shakedown, however, until you sign."

3. Explain that the project will be frozen upon receipt of approval. Any additional work—change, addition, or system maintenance—will require a new DPSR.

Now, we can end a job. Once we have user sign-off, it's over, and our customer should be aware of this. Of course, we are not pushing anyone off a high bridge into a strong wind. If the user needs modifications, we still must provide such service. We are simply going to do so in a more businesslike manner.

In the previous example showing our problems with change requests, I was your user, Martha Mitchell. I called you, asking that the date be moved from the right-hand side to the left, and you expressed your willingness to do so. Now, however, one thing changes. My modification request is no longer automatically an extension of the original project. It is a new request, and you ask me to submit it *in writing*.

This buys you three solid advantages:

One, I must give my request more careful thought in order to write it down.

Two, you must begin our entire cycle of communication all over again. You respond with a Confirmation. Then, you prepare a mini-Contract, telling me how long moving the date will take and how much it will cost.

Three, I must agree, in writing, to end result, time, and expense before any work takes place.

Not only is the communication channel wide open between us, but management of people and resources in your area has to improve. Estimating is more accurate, because you are determining the necessary time framework and cost based on an isolated, specifically defined Task. Other, and perhaps more important, assignments are not unexpectedly pressured to a stand-still. You and I both understand what this type of request will involve.

Also, there are two other possible advantages:

One, when I wasn't confronted with time or cost, it was easy to demand almost any modification. Now, you come to me saying it will cost $400 and take three days to move my date. I just may decide I can live with it where it is.

Two, once I realize the time and money required to make changes, I should begin putting more detail into subsequent requests. I will spell out exactly what I require (Put the date on the left. Print only 50 lines.) at the beginning of future projects and services, because I've learned modifications can be more complicated and expensive than initial effort.

This Closure approach is even more crucial to adequate administrative control in our maintenance function. Few, if any, organizations know for sure what it costs to maintain a given system. Neither DP nor users have been able to plan sufficiently for the allocation of time and actual money expended each year on maintenance.

Now, however, we can simplify the maintenance process. We can make *our* definition stick, turning constant crisis into a workable and practical procedure.

Remember, your customer signed a Contract and the Checkpoint documents. He or she agreed to the stipulated system specifications. Maintenance, therefore, *is only that activity necessary to maintain the original specifications.* Programming bugs will surface and must be corrected. Charts and tables may need updating. The system must adhere to changing State or Federal Regulations. You notice, however, that during the maintenance effort, the specifications do *not* change. Any request that adds to, deletes from, or changes the accepted specifications is not maintenance. It is a new request and is handled as we discussed on page 89.

Maintenance then, based on the initial system specs, becomes a separate DPSR. It is efficiently processed through a maintenance Contract, renewable on an annual basis. Time is projected and costs are figured—just as for any other request.

Some corporations have gone a step further. They now break out their maintenance function into a separate unit. This maintenance group works solely on Contracts initiated by maintenance DPSRs. With this approach, organizations can identify manpower allocation and time required for maintenance of each system in operation. Both data processors and the user develop better yearly budgets.

There is also a side benefit to renewing a maintenance Contract annually. Every company seems to have at least one user who is clinging tenaciously to an outdated system. The thing clunks along in the basement—slow-running, inefficient, and almost impossible to maintain. Perhaps no one from DP is even current in the programming language involved, so God forbid the thing should hang. The system does run, however, and the user does not want it touched.

Where maintenance Contracts come up for annual renewal, you have a shot at bringing horse-and-buggy systems into the jet age. Suppose you go to your user at maintenance Closure for one year and explain that maintenance of his system for the next year will cost $8,000. (You have to import a consultant from Vermont every time the thing bombs.) Why not also demonstrate that your customer can have a new and better system for $4,000 in development costs? Then show him that once his system is updated, he will probably only pay $2,000 annually for system maintenance. Such a presentation of specifics is convincing. Even the most intractable users opt for modernization, making your overall job easier.

4. Reaffirm Shakedown with your user. Be sure the planned Shakedown period is still adequate.

This, of course, is necessary only if you employ Shakedown in your organization. I must add, however, for those of you not currently using the Shakedown approach, that I highly recommend trying it.

Shakedown is a period of time in which individuals from DP remain on tap to assist the user in system or service utilization. Services provided range from a hot-line telephone for questions and emergencies to actual placement of data processors in the user environment.

In project development, Shakedown is often the seventh or final Phase. In methods and procedures or other areas, it is set for the date the customer begins to use the service provided. In all areas, Shakedown elicits excellent feedback as to what works and what doesn't work for the customer. For example, one especially valuable application is in simulation, where end result is often several months removed from the initial effort. Shakedown puts someone from the simulation group on the scene when a model is being tested. Apart from helping the user, he has the opportunity to evaluate his unit's success or failure first-hand.

No matter how Shakedown is used, cost and time are estimated by DP and agreed to by the customer. Closure, then, is the time to review projections for Shakedown to ensure they are still reasonable.

One problem I've noted is that Shakedown periods are often too long, leaving the door open for unnecessary do-it-yourself system enhancement. Another problem is that Shakedown is too easily confused with parallel test. The two are not the same. In systems development, Shakedown during System Test is generally inconclusive and must be repeated. Successful Shakedown always takes place in a *production* environment. With procedures, Shakedown is only useful once prior methods have been fully replaced or discarded.

Be sure your user understands that Shakedown can only begin *after* he signs the Closure Document. Be sure he also knows the duration of Shakedown and what occurs at its completion. For example, maintenance Contracts become effective the day Shakedown of a system ends.

The Shakedown approach has generated good results. Data processors gain a different perspective of the customer's needs when they must help him use what DP produces. This more involved viewpoint often improves action on future requests. Shakedown also can cut back the total number of change requests. Users can't use our services to their best advantage if they don't know for sure what they have. The traditional reaction has been, "It doesn't work," not, "I don't understand it." The logical next step has been, "Since it doesn't work, change it." With Shakedown, we help customers appreciate the possibilities inherent in any system or service. We help them comprehend and accept limitations. As a result, everything appears to work better, and the user finds far fewer things to change.

5. Enclose a copy of the original DPSR or request.

This is purely an educational exercise. Consider the value of a user's seeing the contrast between his simple, initial request and the complex monster it has probably become.

Such an illustration has to bolster his acceptance of any time slippage or cost overrun. It also helps convince any customer to define his requirements more completely at the initiation of subsequent requests.

6. Express appreciation to individuals from the customer department, where appropriate.

In the Closure of a small project or service, a simple thank-you to cooperative liaisons and others should be included. In more formal situations—such as the Closure of a large-scale project—recognition documents are written separately. They are, however, distributed at the same time as the Closure Memorandum or Report. (See "Congratulate where appropriate," page 48.)

One caution. If you have not had a good relationship with your user, skip it. He knows your true attitude as well as you do. Nothing sounds more insincere or sarcastic than

> "We want to thank you and your people for all you did to contribute to our joint success."

when neither side has spoken kindly to each other for six months.

7. Include all necessary information—test results, scheduling, maintenance arrangements, contact in operations, etc.

Use good judgment and provide whatever is necessary for your customer to get full benefit from a system or service in your Closure document. Don't wait for questions to arise or problems to develop. Be sure your user has illustrative material to review if possible. Assure his access to individuals or groups who can respond immediately to any area of customer concern.

DP is highly specialized. Depending on his problem, it generally takes a user three or four telephone calls to locate help. This is not direct communication. It's a hodge-podge of "I don't know" and "perhaps you could," frustration to the customer and death to data processing credibility.

Even worse, our time is too often spent going "round Robin's barn" with a user over a situation we can't deal with anyway. For example, if you're in development and your customer's system goes down or he has a scheduling conflict, do you want the call? If you're in operations and programming problems turn up in a system, do you want to field the user's complaints?

Provide a contact for your customer should any of a list of potential difficulties occur. You know, from past experience, where troubles most often originate. Anticipate for your user.

List names, areas of expertise, and telephone numbers. If actual name is hard to pinpoint in your organization, or you feel it may change, at least provide the appropriate number to call. One that will get your user into the proper department or unit. Remember, as long as he only has yours, you're going to get the call—probably at three o'clock in the morning.

This type of service-orientation at Closure makes life easier on everyone. Certainly, the user is better able to handle problems and, therefore, easier to deal with personally. Relationships also improve between the data processing groups. Have you ever wandered through an operations area and listened to the comments on the ancestry of the programming staff? Perhaps you have discussed operators with programmers? The opinions are rarely complimentary. Only better problem dispersal—through improved communication—can change some of these attitudes. Each group needs to understand the work situation of the others. Each group, users included, must recognize that a person can and wants to cope with *only* his legitimate responsibilities.

8. Ensure proper distribution.

Closure documents travel the same path as the Contract and any Checkpoint vehicles—both the signed copies and necessary "informational" distribution.

Again, check for any individuals or groups whose names or telephone extensions are appearing for the first time, especially in element 7. Be sure they also receive a copy.

* *

Here are the important techniques from SIX KEYS TO SUCCESS:

1. Don't be "iffy."

This document is a *Closure*. If you're "iffy" here, you will be stuck with the same open-ended game plan that has plagued data processing since its inception.

2. Be specific.

Being specific is particularly crucial in two elements:

One, when explaining procedures for submitting change requests or obtaining system maintenance after Closure, be specific. Vagueness here can only convince your customer that you're slamming a door. He may even be reluctant to give you a sign-off because of his uncertainty about receiving additional service.

Two, when providing information and contacts for your user in case of a problem situation, link names and numbers to specific customer requirements:

"Call Joe O'Reilly—ext. 444—for scheduling information."

Otherwise, users continue to frustrate themselves and you by calling the wrong people or departments.

3. Write to make friends.

The tone of all subsequent communication between DP and the customer is set in the Closure document. Avoid ever suggesting the disinterested: "Don't call us. We'll call you." No user wants to feel that your concern ends at completion. No data processor can afford to put his customer so on the defensive, especially since future association is a certainty.

* *

Sample Project or Service Completion Memo—The Closure

Like the Systems or Service Contract, this document cannot easily be practiced in a hypothetical situation. Required information and acceptable format will vary greatly, depending on the size and complexity of the customer's request.

Again, however, you can test your ability to institute completion by reviewing a Closure document as if you were the user involved. Once you recognize what you would need as the reader, you have a solid basis for any Completion Report you prepare.

If you remember our Department Highlights, Denis Jacques took over as Project Co-ordinator for Mitchell's project. Let's assume that work is completed and Denis has composed a Closure with the following information:

PROJECT COMPLETED, MEETING SPECIFICATIONS AS OUTLINED IN CONTRACT AND MODIFIED IN PHASE COMPLETION REPORTS.

PLEASE FORWARD APPROVAL BY JULY 26.

MAINTENANCE WILL BE THE RESPONSIBILITY OF MARY MCCARTHY, DP MAINTENANCE UNIT, EXT. 418.

ANY MODIFICATIONS NECESSARY IN FUTURE SHOULD BE SENT TO ME IN WRITING (A NEW DPSR).

THANK YOU.

Would you—as the customer—be willing to accept your system as presented?

* *

You may have decided to sign-off. If the end result is good, you might even formalize your approval for Denis without too many questions.

Denis did, however, leave out a number of crucial elements—areas of information that could strengthen his present case and some that are bound to create future problems.

For example:

1. Reader comprehension

We have said many times that we would always enclose illustrative material, where possible. Anything that helps a reader *visualize* encourages understanding and acceptance.

Denis told you the project was complete, but he did not show you, even though he easily could have. Using "interruption" technique, he might have enclosed a copy of final test results, thereby relating finished product directly to your original request.

Certainly, in any Closure document, you would expect to find completion date and cost. This is especially important when either one or both vary from the initial estimates. Contrast between the original and the actual could be graphically depicted—and often easily explained—simply by Denis's including a copy of the original DPSR. This way, the user sees the difference immediately between his beginning assumptions and what was actually required to meet his needs.

2. Future assistance

Did you recognize *your* responsibility in obtaining maintenance for your system, or did you think Mary McCarthy would automatically take over? Remember, systems maintenance is now a separate DPSR (renewed annually), and DPSRs generally originate with the customer.

As our assumption throughout our examples has been that Mitchell is a new user, Denis could have helped by including a completed maintenance DPSR for the first year. This would have reassured you—as Mitchell—of continuity in DP support. It also would have performed an educational function, providing guidelines so you could handle this requirement in the future. Of course, Denis also would have to explain any other necessary procedures, and ask you to submit the maintenance DPSR to Mary by the required date.

Even if you are an experienced user, Denis should have jogged your memory. Many customers are still uneasy with the fact that a system going into production is *their* system, not DP's. Helping these users feel confident of their ability to secure future service makes them far more willing to let go now.

In either case, Denis must spell out the timetable. Imagine your reaction to future requests for a sign-off once you've had the experience of sitting in limbo—lost between the conclusion of the development effort and the beginning of the maintenance function.

You also were told that any future modifications should be sent to Denis in writing. This is correct. Did you, however—as a user—have any mental questions as to what he meant by "modifications"? In order to make DP's definition of maintenance stick, each customer must fully understand the distinction between change requests and maintenance responsibility.

Denis had the opportunity to ensure reader comprehension in his original directives:

"Maintenance of the *accepted* system will be the responsibility of . . . ."

"Any future change to the *established* system specifications is a new request and should be sent to me in writing (a new DPSR)."

Another concern here, of course, is tone. No user should ever suspect he hears a door slamming. Denis could have sounded service-oriented while still insisting on proper procedure. All he had to do was to show the user some open doors:

"If you wish, Mary will be happy to discuss the full maintenance cycle with you."

"I'll be glad to help you evaluate any modifications you feel should be considered."

With many customers, the more sure they are of help when they need it, the less they need it.

3. Praise

If Denis is going to thank you at all, wouldn't you prefer he be more specific?

For instance, is he just thanking you or is "you" plural, to include your staff? If so, people like to see their names, providing personal recognition.

What exactly is he thanking you for? He can hardly hope to motivate appropriate behavior on subsequent assignments if he doesn't tell you now *what* actions were most appreciated.

Being specific about "who" should share the credit and detailing "what" actually prompted a thank-you also makes any expression of praise sound more genuine. A blanket "thanks" is a cliche. The definitive "Thanks, Mitch, for all the working weekends" is sincere.

4. Shakedown

The work on Mitchell's request was done on a 4 Phase approach, so Shakedown is

not automatically included. Denis could have offered a Shakedown period, however, as an additional service—including, of course, time involved and cost to the
user.

This is often done on small assignments if there is any question of customer
understanding or acceptance of the completed project. Just remember, if
Shakedown is proposed in a Closure document, the user must be asked to agree to
it in writing and by a specific date.

5. Customer sign-off

Denis did ask you—as Mitchell—for approval of the total project by July 26.
Would it be to his advantage to strengthen this request?

Insecure or inexperienced customers sometimes delay, giving themselves or
their management additional time to evaluate results. Other users occasionally
attempt to institute last-minute changes as a condition of granting approval.

Denis needs to give you—the customer—a motive of self-interest, not only for
meeting his timetable, but for giving him any sign-off at all.

Suppose he changed his request to:

"Please let me have your approval by July 26, so we can release your system to
Operations in time for your first scheduled production run on September 1."

Now you know that if you take beyond July 26 to sign, you may miss your
anticipated production date. Denis has also subtly informed you that your system
will not go into production at all unless approved.

I think you'll sign.

* *

Let's try restructuring this Project Closure or Completion document to include
more information and introduce better tone.

SUBJECT: Product Liability Outstanding Losses
DPSR# EX1992, PCN# 668
Project Closure or Phase IV Completion Report

1. P.L.O.L. project completed (date) at a cost of (amount), meeting specifications as
   outlined in Systems Contract and modified in Phase Completion Reports. (See test
   results, Exhibit 1.)

2. Please forward your approval of the completed system to me by July 26, so we can
   release P.L.O.L. to Operations in time for your first scheduled production run on
   September 1.

3. Maintenance of the accepted system will be the responsibility of Mary McCarthy, DP
   Maintenance Unit, ext. 418. She will need a maintenance DPSR by (date). (See
   enclosed, Exhibit 2.)

4. If you wish, Mary will be happy to review the full maintenance cycle with you.

5. Any future changes to the established system specifications will be treated as a new request and should be sent to me in writing (a new DPSR).

6. I'll be glad to help you evaluate any modifications you feel should be considered.

7. Mitch, I especially want to thank you and your liaison, Tom Fitzgerald, for all your cooperation. I have never seen test data developed in such record time. Thanks also to Jean Blair for all the background information she researched during our System Survey.

8. If I can provide any further assistance, just call—ext. 203.

Sign-off copies: Manager, DP Area or Company
Manager, Customer Area or Company

Informational copies: Liaison, Customer Area or Company
Ultimate Users (if applicable)
Supporting Departments—DP and Customer Individuals mentioned first in this document
Systems Review Committee (if applicable)
Anyone else on original Contract distribution

****

This sample Closure is informal in tone and highly personalized. It is deliberately designed to build bridges between you and customers you deal with regularly. Other Completion documents may, of course, be more formal or structured. Format and sequence must suit the size of a project or service and the number and type of people involved.

Whatever style of Closure you write in your organization, just be sure that both your administrative requirements and your customer's need for service are satisfied.

REPORT WRITING

The term you will hear most frequently in data processing is *result-oriented reports*. Generally written and distributed as memorandums, these documents are not the dry collection of facts we so often find gathering dust on corporate bookshelves. Instead, they present a solid analysis of a situation or problem, including suggested action or possible alternatives. Their primary function is to facilitate realistic administrative decision making. Result-oriented reports project and evaluate *end result*.

This type of report has become so crucial to vigorous leadership that many organizations now hire outside consultants, like myself, to prepare them. I'm glad to do it. Writing such reports is a good source of consulting revenue. However, importing outside talent is not necessarily the best way to get comprehensive and meaningful reports for two important reasons:

One, any consultant, including myself, who comes into your department to compose a report can only begin by picking your brains. No one can know your working environment—your job—as well as you do.

Two, once the report is completed, I pick up my check and go home. All I care about is that the document is well-written enough to assure me future assignments. I do not care what management decisions are made based on my recommendations.

Who should care? Who is going to have to implement or at least live with such decisions? You know more than I do. You have a greater personal stake in the management process. You are the logical choice to prepare result-oriented reports for your administration.

Why do organizations go to consultants for report preparation? The traditional rationale has been that consultants provide an objective outsider's viewpoint. Certainly, this is valuable in the initial consideration of any work situation or problem. Too often, however, consultants do not get to "consult" with any inside people in a cooperative framework. The final report remains exclusively an outside interpretation, making everyone affected view the end result as a "hatchet" operation. Perhaps you've seen this happen. Compliance with the administrative decisions reached is usually reluctant and minimal. No one, manager, employee, or consultant, is satisfied.

Why, then—again—do organizations not even allow their employees to assist consultants in preparing reports, let alone encourage them to write such documents on their own? The answer is simple. *Most of the reports written fully or partially in-house are lousy.* They're long, rambling political devices, with little clarity and a great deal of CYA. I once saw an in-house report that ran an impossible 85 pages. Sadly, someone had invested two months of his life, only to have this company call me in to cut it down to 5 pages.

This is not to say DP people within a corporation cannot write reports. You can. It does suggest that many of you dislike writing reports, considering the task tedious and time-consuming. It also suggests you may not be seeing good decisions result from your efforts. Each time this happens, of course, your motivational level is lowered in a never-ending vicious circle. The report writing experience has turned off many a data processor.

Fortunately, result-oriented reports do not have to be difficult to write. They also can be highly persuasive to any management. All that is required is a knowledge of the mental approach and techniques professional report writers employ.

18

The Systematic Approach to Report Preparation

The best way to begin learning effective report writing is a logical progression of "mental" steps—each simplifying the next in the process. (See Exhibit D.)

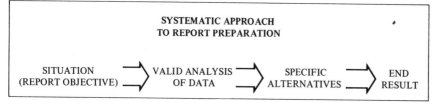

SYSTEMATIC APPROACH
TO REPORT PREPARATION

SITUATION (REPORT OBJECTIVE) ⟹ VALID ANALYSIS OF DATA ⟹ SPECIFIC ALTERNATIVES ⟹ END RESULT

Exhibit D

The first step is the definition of objective, the *what* of a report. Why are you preparing it? What makes it necessary?

Many people do not attempt such a determination until during the analytical process. I find trying to pin down purpose while evaluating data sends me off on continual tangents. Try defining objective first and then move through a valid analysis of the available facts. You may wish to modify your original objective as you proceed, but at least you have a starting point. You are viewing all data in light of parameters already established. The entire analytical process, including the determination of what are pertinent data and what are not, can actually be cut in half.

As you proceed with your analysis, you draw conclusions and recommendations, based on fact and on predetermined objective. You are linking each conclusion and recommendation not only to supporting data, but to the specific situation that prompted the entire report.

I prefer to think of conclusions and recommendations as alternatives. The very words—conclusion and recommendation—convey a sense of positive one-sidedness. Come up with alternatives, and you are forcing yourself to think in terms of action *both pro and con.*

Any number of report writers conclude here. They make their suggestions, present their analytical response, and get out. This is not result-oriented reporting.

In order for intelligent administrative decisions to be made, each alternative must be dropped into context or *end result*. Readers must know the projected value and/or disadvantage of any proposed action.

Use the Systematic Approach to Report Writing and any Management Report goes down on paper easier and faster. Also, the report you distribute will be a good one. For example, following each step in the sequence approach helps you solve the four primary problems confronting any report writer:

1. Getting the reader's full attention

The stumper with most reports is that they are *not* read. No other document is as frequently skimmed or ignored as the Management Report.

Your first step then in beginning an effective reporting process is to determine *what makes your report important to your reader(s)*. What will prompt your audience to review your report carefully and take your conclusion seriously? Define the reader's personal involvement and you have a "starting point" for successful presentation of your own interests and recommendations.

Also, you must consider the visual impact of your proposed document. Bulky or unwieldy reports look boring. Brief reports, containing only pertinent information, encourage attentiveness. Well-thought-out titles and subheadings, in the reader's frame of reference, will cause any browser to stop and examine your material.

No report is of any value sitting in someone's in-box. It must be read to be acted upon.

2. Establishing reader comprehension

I see many reports originating in data processing areas that are so technical or complex, few besides the writers could hope to understand them. Unfortunately, these documents are generally intended to "sell" DP recommendations to a user or corporate committee.

We have discussed people's reaction to something they don't understand. It's *negative*. Lack of clarity defeats and distorts the most positive facts and examples.

Also, each reader of a result-oriented report must understand your objective in preparing the report in the first place. If you explain your purpose as well as your content, you get your readers on your wavelength. They are able to view the report's data and resulting conclusions in the same context in which you viewed them.

Any report's original objective and actual content should be clearly defined from the beginning.

3. Writing convincingly

To present an assortment of facts is not sufficient. Readers of result-oriented reports rely on your analytical judgment for assistance in making valid management decisions.

Too often, Management Reports only suggest courses of action in the form of recommendations. This does not necessarily produce a climate of acceptance. A convincing presentation increases reader awareness, not only of proposed action, but the consequences of not taking such action. Your reader must know the possibilities if he does and the certainties if he doesn't. Called the "between a rock and a hard place" approach, this makes any reader more prone to at least *try* your solutions. It is the only recognized cure for administrative indecision.

4. Obtaining results

The most important part of any reporting process is the *end result* it produces. Everything in a Management Report should be geared to evoking specific action.

One way to ensure response is to make all recommendations explicit and detailed. The easier you make it for your reader to do as you propose, the more likely he is to cooperate.

Another crucial element is time. Most in-house reports need to link recommendation to *time framework*. Suggested actions should convey a sense of urgency or even actual need.

Many report writers have been sandbagged by management waiting too long. By the time the original recommendations from a report are implemented in some organizations, they're outdated. They then bomb, not because they were invalid, but because the situation they were developed to combat has changed in the interim.

Always tell your reader the "expiration" date of any recommendation. Where possible, tell him *why* action is necessary prior to that date and all bets are off after it. This not only encourages more rapid decisions, but it clears you if your readers stall.

Remember, management procrastination is a decision—usually the wrong one.

19
Techniques of Professional Report Writers

Here are the techniques and tips consultants use in preparing better Management Reports.

1. Brevity.

Result-oriented reports are a management tool. Brevity enables your reader(s) to use this tool with a minimal investment of time and effort. Be as brief as possible, without sacrificing reader comprehension or your personal credibility.

A. Condense.

We all believe we only include what's necessary. I know, however, how possessive I can be about material I worked hard to obtain. Perhaps you feel the same way?

If I have plenty of data, I am tempted to include it all, hoping my reader will be impressed, if not overwhelmed. Can't you hear him saying to himself, "What a fantastic research job she's done"?

Unfortunately, my great research has produced a welter of irrelevant detail which is now obscuring the important points I hoped to make. "Less is more" in any Management Report, and here's a rule of thumb to achieve it almost painlessly:

If any piece of data cannot be used to illustrate a specific conclusion or recommendation, throw it out. Interesting as it may be, it's extraneous to your primary objective.

The reverse is also true: If any alternative you hoped to present cannot be supported by facts you've assembled, throw it out. It may be something you've wanted to say for some time. It may even be something that needs to be said, but it does not belong in *this* report.

B. Use graphics.

Illustrations of all kinds—charts, tables, graphs—have always been a part of the Management Report. They usually, however, have been relegated to the Appendix.

Now, any simple graphic material *that takes the place of prose,* thereby cutting back verbiage, is placed directly in the body of your report. This keeps reports shorter and makes exhibits less complicated to use.

It is also perfectly acceptable in contemporary business to be creative with your graphics. One example I saw concerned a workspace allocation report. A DP department was moving from one location to another and an individual was assigned to report on space dispersal. If you have ever seen a standard report on this subject, you know how impossible it can be.

"Two feet beyond the terminal and up six feet is wall clock X . . . ." Or, they present squared-off boxes, representing floor space with X's and Y's—all out of scale—indicating people and equipment placement.

Not this report. The person involved took his camera to the new location and took pictures. On each picture, he noted exact arrangement of work areas and equipment. Every reader could *visualize* exactly what the new location looked like and how it could be used. Movement of the entire department was fast and smoothly organized. That report was "workable"—our prime criterion for judging a business document—and it earned its author a Performance Bonus.

I do have one caution concerning the use of illustrative material, however. If you are not artistically inclined, leave the preparation of your graphics to someone who is. Nothing detracts from the professionalism of a Management Report any faster than a lopsided stick figure or smudged ink sketch. Almost every organization has a graphic arts, audiovisual, advertising, marketing, or printing service area. Use it. If your company does not, enlist the aid of an associate whose artistic talents exceed your own.

C. Use titles and subheadings.

We discussed the contribution of titles and subheadings to easy reading and effective document organization. We also considered the importance of making each title or subheading pertinent to the section it describes, avoiding such say-nothing abstractions as PURPOSE, DEFINITION, and SCOPE.

Now, let's impose limits in terms of numbers. I have yet to see a successful result-oriented report that contained more than *five* main headings. More than five, and you are either being redundant or attempting to cover too much ground in one report. The only possible exceptions would be a full-scale Feasibility Study or a major Proposal. Each of these could run up to, but should contain no more than, *ten* main topic listings.

Under each main heading, well-organized reports present only *four* or fewer subheadings. Again, if you wind up with more, you either are being repetitive or you need to more carefully define the main heading involved. Long lists of subheadings are the best indication that a main heading is vague or ill-conceived.

D. Use the Appendix wisely.

Don't be afraid of the Appendix, and don't abuse it. Many report writers avoid using an Appendix altogether. Others employ it as a dumping ground for material they couldn't find space for in the body of their report.

Remember, of course, that any complex or highly technical charts or graphs still belong in the Appendix. This is also true of any illustration your reader will expect to use *apart from* your cover report. (See "Make paragraphs flow logically," page 62.)

Be sure to use your Appendix for any consideration of past studies or any required analysis of data sampling collection techniques. For example, suppose I prepared a report on utilization of available hardware in my organization. I would put descriptive information about the software packages used in my monitoring in the Appendix. Readers who want to know where my figures came from will look for and read such detail there. Other readers may not need to know or wouldn't understand the technical considerations anyway. Why should they be forced to wade through methodology in the body of my report?

2. Encourage reader interest.

Most managers approach the reading of a report with a sigh of resignation. No one expects to be caught up in or excited by a report's content.

The only way to change this "necessary evil" attitude is to write reports that involve each reader directly. Any administrator who finds *his* concerns reflected in a report's overall content is going to be interested in the conclusions and recommendations presented. He may not agree with them, but he is certain to pay attention.

A. Start with a "grabber."

We do this with other types of documents. Why not grab the reader in a Management Report, sparking reader curiosity from the beginning? (See "Be aware of sentence construction," page 61.)

Traditional business reports have been slow starters. Readers could skim volumes and not miss much of importance. It's no wonder reader attention to most reports has been casual at best.

"Grabbers" change this. For example, I recently saw a Management Report dealing with ineffective assignment of manpower. The opening statement was dynamite:

"The Data Processing Department does not need to hire any new personnel next year."

The writer, of course, went on to explain. Acquisition of new personnel could not be justified, because the department was not fully utilizing people already available. That's pretty dry material. If you were in that area, however, and screaming for more help, wouldn't you read the report? Consider the difference in your interest level between this writer's opening statement and the PURPOSE, DEFINITION, and SCOPE routine.

I saw another report on the same subject that employed a rhetorical question opener. It began:

"Are ETAs impossible to meet?"

The writer then proceeded to answer his own question. He demonstrated that target dates were impossible because of failure to allocate manpower properly. His material may have been the same old thing, but his readers were already hooked. Anyone in his department who had blown an ETA read his report carefully and thoroughly. Check that response with the one he would have evoked with

"The purpose of this report is to investigate personnel allocation over the period covering . . . ."

For most readers, there is no comparison.

B. Present the opposing view and drawbacks, if any.

Opposition is a strong reader reaction. Certainly, disagreement with the suggested recommendations in a report is better than no response at all. In fact, reader resistance is often the starting point for productive consideration of a problem. It prompts the negotiation necessary to finding a solution.

Where possible, anticipate any negative thinking on the part of your reader(s). Confront it head-on in your original report. Readers are never blasé about their potential veto power. They read carefully to catch your acknowledgment of their involvement. They also look to determine if their reservations concerning your subject received fair play.

Remember, ignoring reader reluctance does not make it go away. Acknowledging it may allow you to answer questions or objections without frustrating follow-up discussion.

C. Use case studies and direct quotes.

Case studies have been around a long time in Management Reports. Yet, few newer techniques make a theoretical proposition more relevant to a reader than a factual story illustrating its application. Just be sure your readers know enough detail about the episode to evaluate its pertinence. "My experience with the XYZ system indicates . . ." is not enough. You must explain what experience, for how long, and the incident that actually occurred and influenced your current recommendation.

Direct quotes are a more recent development in result-oriented reporting. Their acceptance grew as people's experience with actual situations became as important to solving DP problems as any verifiable data.

Interviewing is now a basic tool of report writing. When you conduct interviews, you may quote individuals directly. Certainly, you would only quote experts in a given field, and their viewpoint can lend credence and emphasis to your conclusion.

One caution with direct quotation. Always tell the person you plan to quote him *at the time of the initial interview*. Some individuals do not wish to be quoted under any circumstances and they don't like surprises. If possible, allow those you do quote to view your report prior to its distribution. If this is impossible, be sure that each receives an "informational" copy.

3. Avoid writing in the third person.

Data processing inherited an objective, third person report style from scientific and academic predecessors. In it, no writer ever intruded his personality into the presentation of material. Facts, and *only* facts, were acceptable.

This approach is no longer possible, given the intended usage of result-oriented reports. By the very act of preparing a Management Report, the writer is participating in the administrative decision-making process. In many instances, his daily activities or future career could be affected by the decision reached, and this has to influence his position. He is not, and cannot pretend to be, an innocent bystander shielded from responsibility by reams of data.

Stepping out of the third person can be uncomfortable. It puts the writer—his analysis and attitudes—on the line. We must do it, however, if result-oriented reports are going to be practical assists to effective management. The easiest way to present your standpoint, without loss of objectivity, is to identify each aspect of the analytical process. Unless you establish these definitions—for yourself as well as your reader—you could find yourself on constantly shifting ground.

A. Carefully distinguish what is data, personal interpretation of data, and writer viewpoint.

Everyone, especially statisticians, knows data can be manipulated. Don't do so in a Management Report. Always present quantitative facts and figures in an easily understood and straightforward format.

How, though, does the reader know that what he sees is actual fact? Well, *data,* by definition, are verifiable. Simply *identify your source,* usually in the Appendix. Your reader now knows that the referenced statement is not open to question. If he wishes to perform the same research you did, he will come up with exactly the same information.

On the other hand, *personal interpretation of data* is always subjective. This does not lessen its value to valid analysis, but it must be explained to the reader. A writer's individual interpretation usually is expressed as a conclusion leading to a suggested recommendation. Each reader should recognize that conclusion's dependency on the experience, background, and current responsibility level of the writer or someone he interviewed.

Remember, also, that personal interpretation of data, unlike data itself, is open to reader question or disagreement. Anticipate any such problems in your original presentation.

Writer viewpoint is more difficult to pin down. Generally, it reflects the context in which the topic of the report was evaluated. It also mirrors the writer's values and priorities and the weight he attributes to certain facts. These influencing factors must be distingusihed from data, as they are the most common source of "ax grinding" or slanted personal interpretation.

For example, suppose a management committee assigns me a report. The recommendations I come up with are good ones, yet each will increase the responsibility and importance of my unit. Unless I acknowledge these side benefits in my original report, any reader might suspect the recommendations are more *writer viewpoint* than accurate analysis. If I point out my personal involvement, however, without waiting to be challenged on it, my ideas must be evaluated solely on overall merit.

B. Balance facts with personal judgment. Add your own comments where appropriate.

When you prepare a Management Report, *you speak as an expert.* With some reports—Feasibility Study or Projected Objectives, for example—you know more than your readers and your opinions are crucial. In fact, your familiarity with a topic will occasionally have more influence on the final decision than any available data.

Here's an illustration. I was once asked to write a report evaluating a particular software package. I had "facts" up to my ears. The vendor had seen to that. I also had demonstrated need. The customers of the DP area were most enthusiastic. Everything—cost, capability, support—looked great.

Unfortunately for the vendor, I had done some work for a firm that had already purchased this package and I knew its failings. The vendor used his customers as testers, compatability had been exaggerated—you know the routine. Therefore, in my report, I listed the "data," only to follow it with a definitive erasure, *"however . . . ."* My client did not buy.

Which was more important to a good management decision in this instance—available data or my personal judgment?

C. Acknowledge any interpretation of data or viewpoint not your own.

It's all too easy to pick up other people's judgments or viewpoints almost through osmosis. This is particularly true if you interview while doing your research. This kind of mental plagiarism is unintentional, but please avoid any suggestion of it in your reports.

Identify the source of any conclusions or recommendations not your own. This supports your objectivity and strengthens your material. Also, giving credit will prevent your reader from asking questions you may not be able to answer adequately.

Of course, any contributors you reference should be notified prior to distribution. They also should receive an "informational" copy of your final report. (See "The Sly Fox and the Big Brown Bear," page 83.)

4. Convey interest and enthusiasm.

Many a legitimate conclusion or valid recommendation has been vetoed because a writer displayed frustration, anger, or impatience. Poor attitudes are catchy.

Conversely, any Management Report is better received when the writer conveys his own interest in his subject and his personal belief in its value. Enthusiasm is also contagious.

Think of your outlook in any report situation as a self-fulfilling prophecy. Let your reader *feel* your conviction. This makes him more highly motivated. It also encourages him to look for the good in your projected end result, if only to see what all the excitement is about.

A. Write a story.

The five elements of successful fiction—*situation, characters, problem, solution, and resolution*—are also vital to well-written Management Reports. Your reader(s) must know the situation prompting the report, the people concerned, existing problems, proposed solutions, and the end result of implementing the solutions.

Nothing conveys writer involvement in his material better than good story logic. The progression from each story element to another also catches the reader up in the situation. It makes him eager to move to resolution and enthusiastic about his participation in end result.

I am not suggesting that any Management Report will become a book "too good to put down.'' Taking your reader with you on your analytical journey, however, just might encourage him to find your ''story'' as absorbing and important as you do.

B. Think in the positive.

Occasionally, each of us writes a report where the conclusions we document are negative. We wind up saying something should not be done, rather than recommending positive action.

I have learned, through long experience, that expressing a conclusion in the negative can often evoke a negative response. In fact this frequently occurs even when your reader actually agrees with your basic premise.

Many people in the communications field believe it can take a reader up to six times longer to understand a negative statement than a positive one. We all mentally transpose negative statements into the positive, comprehend them, and then transpose back to negative mode. Naturally, this process slows comprehension and may even prevent it. As we've discussed several times, a reader's instinctive reaction to something he doesn't understand is negative. This is why we elicit unreasonable negative responses to our reasonable negative conclusions.

Where possible, express recommendations in the positive. It's easy to do if you employ one simple rule. Always give reasons why something *should* be done and avoid giving reasons why something *should not* be done.

Take this example:

"Revision of present project control procedures are not recommended because of resulting confusion in manpower assignments."

That's a negative statement and can automatically evoke a negative reaction from many readers. Turn it around:

"The current project control procedures simplify manpower assignments and should be maintained."

This says the same thing and yet is much more likely to elicit an affirmative response.

There's also an additional advantage to positive expression. The second version is shorter. Check your own writing. Positive statements usually require fewer words. Now, two things are working to help the reader understand and accept your recommendation—no confusing negatives and shorter sentences overall.

C. Avoid formality.

The traditional formal approach to report writing is not always the most effective in result-oriented reporting. It can suggest a reserved attitude or total detachment on the part of the writer and probably will elicit the same from each reader.

Wherever possible, give your readers the benefit of a conversational tone. Some formality may be required, depending on the type of report, your subject matter, and your audience. Generally, however, an informal approach conveys greater writer concern and encourages more direct reader participation.

5. make a convincing presentation.

Being objective does not eliminate the need to be convincing in the presentation of recommendations and conclusions. A result-oriented report should *influence* management decisions as well as provide information. Take a stand, but do so skillfully, without obvious politicking or overaggressiveness.

A. Consider climate and past history.

Investigate thoroughly the climate in which your recommendation will be circulated. For example, is it a year of financial austerity in your organization? Has there been a shake-up of management, resulting in new policies and priorities? Are you leading from a position of strength—good performance, with minimal time slippage and cost overrun—or has your credibility slipped with your customers and management?

All of these factors influence the preconceived notions and mental attitude of your readers. Determine this "atmosphere" before you write. Knowledge of your readers' orientation allows you to develop recommendations that make sense to their *current* way of thinking.

Also, consider the past history of your report topic. What was the fate of prior recommendations on the same or a similar subject? Why did they succeed, if they did? Which ones failed? How has the situation changed, if at all? In this way, you avoid nonproductive duplication of effort and are prepared, in advance, to counter objections.

B. Provide full information.

A reader can properly evaluate conclusions and recommendations only if he knows all the facts and individuals involved. Merge complete information with active sentence tone to assist reader understanding and elicit agreement.

Take these sample sentences from reports I reviewed:

"The proposed system was suggested to the Data Processing Department by the Accounting Department."

This statement is passive in tone. It also leaves out essential identification of the responsible individuals in both areas.

"The Accounting Department suggested the system to Data Processing."

This has active tone, but still provides insufficient detail.

"Michael Buckley, supervisor in the Accounting Department, contacted Barbara Jacobs, Director of new projects in Data Processing. He requested development of a system to provide a quarterly corporate income listing."

Now, the reader has all the facts. He understands who originated the request, who received it, and what the request entails.

Please note that when you are providing adequate background, the shortest version is not always the best. Brevity is important, of course, but it should not be attained by omitting information the reader needs.

C. Eliminate bias.

It's hard to stay totally objective in result-oriented reporting, particularly if the subject matter is of critical concern to you or your unit. Even a *suggestion* of bias, however, can weaken any Management Report. The best way to avoid conveying a lack of objectivity is to eliminate or modify any section of your report beginning with these sentences:

"While perhaps not directly related to this report . . . ."

This is an immediate tip-off to all readers that you have something you've been wanting to say for a long time. They now also know you are going to use this report as a soapbox and lay it on them.

If material is "not directly related to this report," leave it out. All you can accomplish by including it is to send your readers off on a tangent, distracting them from your actual report objectives.

"As I stressed previously . . . ."

Here is a dangerous approach. It puts any reader on the defensive and, as we have discussed, people on the defensive are incapable of learning anything. In order for your reader now to agree with your premise, he must admit—at least mentally—that he was *wrong* before. How many individuals in your organization are quick to do that? Certainly, the one hold-out on a management committee is not going to do so in the midst of his peers. He'll go to the wall defending his original position.

I know it is occasionally important to point out that a subject has come up before. Do so, however, without provoking rationalization or excuses. "As we discussed previously . . . " at least conveys a cooperative exchange. Only you and perhaps one of your readers will know it was a "bang your shoe on the table" type of discussion.

"Since action was not taken . . . ."

This is the classic, finger-pointing assignment of blame. How productive can it be to aim it directly at those you must "sell" on your recommendations? Believe me, if "action was not taken . . . " before, using this tone to say so practically guarantees it will not be taken this time either.

"When you did not respond . . . ."

No one is comfortable with organizational types who play the martyr. The implication here is: "Oh, *poor me*, having to work with shmucks like you who don't even answer their mail. Let me show you how well I coped with the impossible situation *you* created." I bet you can feel yourself getting angry and impatient already. That's your reader's inevitable reaction also.

Actually, such a sentence should not be necessary. When you do not get a response to a Management Report within a reasonable length of time—call. Ask if your reader(s) need additional material. Perhaps they have questions you can answer. This prompts some sort of verbal reply. You then can ask them to confirm their decision or actions in writing.

D. Restate and reinforce your conclusions and recommendations.

Too many Management Reports just seem to drop off into the Appendix. They do not conclude forcefully. Get in the habit of restating, for comprehension, and reinforcing, for motivation, any conclusions and recommendations you've drawn in the context of your material. This summary approach allows you to end your report on the strongest note possible. It gives your reader a handle for the enthusiasm you've generated.

A concise conclusion also can save you considerable writing effort. Most Management Reports are distributed under a cover letter or memorandum. Writing this overview document is difficult, and it doesn't always accurately reflect the full thrust of your analytical judgment. If you conclude with a succinct summary, you can simply lift out that section of your report, making it, with some modification, your cover. No more struggling to compose what needs to be said, without saying too much. Also, you will successfully reach those readers who do not wish to wade through the detail, and read only the introductory letter or memorandum. They now at least are getting a brief exposure to your most critical elements, and staying in tune with readers who review the entire document.

E. Keep your door open.

Actions do speak louder than words. Demonstrate your conviction that your ideas are important by offering help to your reader(s). State your availability to clarify or elaborate any point they may question. Volunteer specific assistance in the implementation of any suggestion you propose.

Nothing more quickly convinces a reader that recommendations are worthwhile than the willingness of their author to get involved and stay involved—beyond putting words on a piece of paper.

20
Report Formats

There are two report formats currently at use in the United States. One is the LOGICAL, the other the PSYCHOLOGICAL.

REPORT FORMATS

LOGICAL
1. INTRODUCTION AND STATEMENT OF PROBLEM
2. DATA
3. DISCUSSION OR ANALYSIS OF DATA
4. CONCLUSIONS
5. SUMMARY WITH RECOMMENDATIONS
6. APPENDIX

PSYCHOLOGICAL
1. INTRODUCTION AND STATEMENT OF PROBLEM
2. CONCLUSIONS AND RECOMMENDATIONS
3. DISCUSSION AND ANALYSIS OF DATA
4. SUMMARY
5. APPENDIX WITH DATA

Don't let the meaning associated with these designations confuse you. The LOGICAL is not necessarily more orderly than the PSYCHOLOGICAL. The PSYCHOLOGICAL is not more emotional than the LOGICAL. They're just names.

Both report formats are functional and easily employed. The LOGICAL is traditional in scientific and technical reporting. I'm sure you've seen it in use. The PSYCHOLOGICAL is newer to result-oriented reporting and increasingly popular in data processing environments for three reasons:

One, it's shorter. Therefore, it is less time-consuming and expensive to write.

Two, it's shorter. Therefore, it is less time-consuming and expensive to read.

Three, it places the bulk of responsibility for analytical judgment on the writer. Most recipients of a PSYCHOLOGICAL report read only to element 2. They want to know *what the problem is* and *what can be done about it,* without having to spend any of their time in investigative effort. They make management decisions solely on the basis of the conclusions and recommendations presented.

This does not mean the writer of a PSYCHOLOGICAL report can slough off on the remaining elements. I find readers who do go on to review the data and its analysis usually have extensive knowledge of the subject. The factual and analytical backup for the conclusions and recommendations must be accurate.

Fortunately, data processors handle the increased responsibility of the PSYCHOLOGICAL approach better than many other professional groups. The nature of our daily work assignments has given us experience in working with data and greater confidence in our personal problem-solving abilities.

Learn to use *both* formats. After defining purpose, the second most important decision any writer makes is which report format to use for a particular report. Let's see if we can determine how such a choice is best made.

Examine the LOGICAL format. What is the most significant element in its structure? What receives the greatest amount of emphasis? Isn't it the data?

If you send me a report in the LOGICAL sequence, I read through the data first. I draw my own conclusions and develop my own recommendations, prior to reading yours. I may even make up my mind completely before reviewing your analysis and not be at all influenced by your judgment.

Now, consider the PSYCHOLOGICAL format. Aren't the conclusions and recommendations the most crucial elements in your presentation? If you send me a report in the PSYCHOLOGICAL, I review your conclusions and recommendations prior to weighing the data. My pondering of the facts has to be influenced by assessments you have already made.

Here, then, is the rule of thumb for determining which report format is best suited to your report objective and your reader's expectations:

If the facts are more important than your analysis of the facts, choose the LOGICAL. If, however, your analysis of the facts is more important than any data, go with the PSYCHOLOGICAL.

Let's take some data processing reports and test our rule:

Feasibility Study or Proposal—which format?

Most in-house documents of this type are written in the LOGICAL. Think, however. In a Feasibility Study or Proposal, what is your reader asking you for? Isn't he looking for the *what, when,* and *how much* of your recommendations and conclusions?

Go one step further. Where did most of the data you're working with in these reports come from? Wasn't it furnished by the user in his initial request or in subsequent interviews and memorandums? He knows the facts. What he needs are the results of your examination of them. Certainly, he doesn't want to wade through information he provided to get to the judgments he must have and cannot accurately make for himself.

Your analysis of the facts is more important than the facts themselves. So, good Feasibility Studies or Proposals are always written in the PSYCHOLOGICAL. Customers get what they want, in a format they can easily use.

Systems Documentation—that's a report—which format?

I'm sure you said LOGICAL, and you're correct. Consider how Documentation is used. Someone must come behind you to fix or enhance what you've done—in effect, modifying your conclusions and recommendations. He or she must know as much about the original situation as you did in order to do the job.

The data are more crucial to effective usage of this report than your analysis. In fact, your analysis will probably be changed by the reader. Consequently, efficient Systems Documentation is written in the LOGICAL.

Forecasting of Personal Objectives—also a report—which format?

With the increasing popularity of management by objective, many of us are confronted with this task, usually on an annual basis. The reports of this type I see most frequently are written in the LOGICAL. Again, however, we must examine our reader's expectations. What are our "objectives"? Aren't they our projection of where we (or our people) are going, based on our analysis of current situation? The goals we're asked to forecast are our conclusions and recommendations. No one else—certainly not our readers—can make the judgments we are being asked to make. They can't know our job and its future direction as well as we do.

Our analysis of the facts, however we define them, is the sole purpose of this report. As a result, Forecasting of Personal Objectives should be presented in PSYCHOLOGICAL format.

Apply this type of questioning to each report you plan to develop. Determine, before writing, which format best suits your report's purpose and the needs of your reader(s). If you have difficulty making a choice, there is one further basis for selection to assist you—the timing of your material. This is not 100% accurate on its own, but works well when used as a final balance on the "facts vs. analysis" scale. Where your subject matter deals with *present need* or *future action,* you probably are better off with the PSYCHOLOGICAL. When you must discuss *past events* or *existing conditions,* consider using the LOGICAL.

There is, by the way, no etched-in-stone law that declares you must use either of these formats exactly as outlined. You can, of course, mix and match elements from each to fit a specific purpose or hit a particular reader's expectations.

For example, if I were to write a report projecting my hardware needs for the coming year, I might modify one of our set formats. I would, of course, start with the PSYCHOLOGICAL as my base—all Forecasting of Objectives is best handled in this format. I could, however, borrow one element from the LOGICAL as follows:

INTRODUCTION AND STATEMENT OF PROBLEM
DATA OR FACTORS BEARING ON PROBLEM
CONCLUSIONS AND RECOMMENDATIONS
DISCUSSION AND ANALYSIS OF DATA
SUMMARY
APPENDIX

This addition provides my reader with crucial stage-setting information. Recall my purpose. I am forecasting hardware requirements in my recommendations and conclusions. My reader must understand current utilization and demand (element 2 from the LOGICAL) *before* he can comprehend and accept my projected requirements.

Occasionally, this kind of rearrangement is highly productive. I do not, however, recommend fooling around with the established formats unless it is absolutely necessary to effective report preparation. For one thing, these formats are accepted universally as presented. They've been employed on a wide variety of reporting topics and proved successful. We know they get the job done.

Another, perhaps better, reason for using them as outlined is the amount of effort and time required to change them. Going with one or the other, without modification, is certainly going to be easier on you. All you have to do is properly select either the LOGICAL or the PSYCHOLOGICAL to get a concise structure for your content.

21

Report Organization—What to Do Before You Write

Anything you can do to avoid rewriting helps make report preparation less tedious. These techniques *organize* your approach to your writing task. They allow you to classify and evaluate available material prior to putting deathless prose on paper. Direction is set. Excess data and unwarranted conclusions or recommendations are eliminated. Proper sequence of your content within the appropriate report format is assured.

1. Write out the main thesis or purpose of your report in one sentence, 20 words or less.

Remember, a report writer's first and most important decision is the definition of objective. Don't make the common mistake of just thinking through your purpose as you begin. It's too easy to be imprecise mentally. Pin yourself down by writing it down. Further discipline yourself by limiting your factual statement to 20 words or less, as this is the optimum length for reader comprehension. Now, you can read it, just as your reader will. You also have a consistent definition available for easy reference throughout the organizational process.

If you cannot write such a sentence to your satisfaction, you certainly are not ready to prepare an entire report. Until you decide exactly what makes your report *necessary,* whatever you write will be inconclusive and unconvincing.

2. Make a list of subject headings.

This is not an outline. It is just a list of the *subject areas* you feel you must cover in your report. Try to arrange the headings in the order you plan to present them.

Check carefully to ensure none are repetitive. Then, critically evaluate your total list to see if any should be more specific or could be combined.

As we discussed earlier, good result-oriented reports, with the exception of Feasibility Studies or Proposals, generally cover no more than five main topics. If you have more than five, go over your entire list again. Cut back to five where possible. If you must have more, be sure each additional subject can be justified. In any event, you should never have more than ten.

Once you are content with your list as arranged, you can complete one final check to ensure the areas enumerated belong in your report. Take each subject heading and bounce it off the sentence defining your thesis or objective. If it doesn't fit exactly—it's tangential or unnecessary, and you can eliminate it.

The best part of this procedure is its relative painlessness. You are simply crossing a one- or two-word subject area off your list. You are not tossing pages of effort in the trash can.

3. Outline the report, noting conclusions and appropriate data.

Some people are able to produce effective Management Reports without outlining. Most people, myself included, cannot. If you are having difficulty with report preparation and are not currently using an outline, I would suggest trying one.

At this point, the process of outlining is easy. You have a concise list of subject areas. Simply expand each into a short, one-sentence main heading. Under each, list any necessary subheadings. Remember, well-organized reports contain only four or fewer subheadings in any category, so restrict yourself to that number. Also, check your subheadings for clarity. Be sure none are repetitious.

Your outline will be even more useful if you go one step further. You have all your facts collected. You have completed your analysis. Once the outline is intact, jot a note to yourself under each subheading. Nothing in detail. Just a one or two word reminder—''Buy hardware. Figures from Joe.'' This indicates the conclusions or recommendations you plan for each section and the data available to support them.

Now check each main heading against your statement of report purpose. You'll be surprised how often expanding a subject area into an outline heading changes its reference. If any main heading does not mesh with your objective, throw it out. You also can eliminate all its associated subheadings and the referenced conclusions and data.

With the remaining pertinent headings, be sure the subheading(s) under each relates exactly. Any subheading that doesn't fit *goes,* along with its noted conclusions and data. This allows you to pare down to the bare bones of a successful report, once again without discarding one paragraph of hard-earned prose.

4. Borrow "briefing" from playscript.

Once their outline is complete, most people feel they are ready to write. After all, they have developed a structural guideline, all of which they know is pertinent to their report objective. Unfortunately, however, two important questions remain that no outline can answer:

One, has any crucial material been left out?

Two, is the proposed content arranged in the most sensible and convincing sequence?

Here you are not checking the selection of one of the two formal report formats discussed earlier. Rather, you are concerned with the progression of your material within each section of either the LOGICAL or the PSYCHOLOGICAL framework.

If these questions are not answered prior to writing, it's easy to get involved in the "delete A, cross out B, insert C" syndrome. You know your outline can take you no further. *Briefing* can.

The briefing technique originated in playscript, a language approach to writing methods and procedures. It's simple to use, and with minor modifications, can be applied to report organization to ensure comprehensive coverage and continuity of presentation. Briefing can also be used whether your original report objective is pro (something should be done) or con (no action is recommended).

Let's say I plan to prepare a pro or positive result-oriented report. My thesis is, "The XYZ Corporation should purchase additional hardware next year." My outline is short:

> I. Additional hardware
>   A. Customer
>   B. Operations
>   C. Speed
>   D. Cost

It looks good. The main heading is concise. My four subheadings appear to be arranged in proper sequence. First are the people-oriented functions of *Customer* and *Operations*. Second, the machine-oriented functions of *Speed* and *Cost*.

Just to be sure, however, I am going to brief before I write. I do so by expanding my main heading into a complete sentence, showing the relationship between the main heading and the proposed content in each subheading. My notations under the subheadings tell me what I planned for each. For example:

I. Additional hardware	I. Additional hardware will
A. Customer	A. facilitate new and larger system required by customer.

B. Operations   B. increase efficiency and
                                 reduce cost in operations.

                                 Additional hardware is

C. Speed   C. faster and more efficient.

D. Cost   D. too costly for the approved
                                 budget.

Now, I can evaluate the structure or sequence of my report in terms of my original thesis. Remember, my report objective is to recommend the purchase of additional hardware. Based on that, is my proposed sequence of material effective?

What about "bad news first"? I am walking out on the most negative note possible. My arrangement of content says to my reader, "Yes, I can do this, this, and this, *but,* I can't afford it". My last subheading, *Cost,* must come first if I am going to use erasure words properly. (See "Put together a convincing message," page 21.)

Also, looking at the briefed outline, am I going to force myself to be repetitive? Certainly, in order to prove my planned statements in subheading A and B, I must first demonstrate increased capability. If *Cost* is now first, *Speed* must be second. Only after I have documented capability can I support the statements I planned in my subheadings *Customer* and *Operations.*

What about their sequence, however? The facts and figures on capability lead sensibly into *Operations,* where the new hardware will actually be used. Only after showing the increased efficiency in *Operations,* can I adequately discuss the contribution of additional hardware to my *Customer*'s requirements.

Briefing then gives me a much more effective outline:

  I. Additional hardware
     A. Cost
     B. Speed
     C. Operations
     D. Customer

Briefing also opens up other avenues of approach. Remember, it's crucial to a report writer to get read. Suppose, looking at the notations on my new outline, I realize my bad news is really bad—say a cost of $4,000,000. Once my reader sees that figure, is he going to read further and recognize the benefits in subheadings B, C, and D? He probably will read only A and have to receive oxygen.

I need to sequence my content so that everything—especially the benefits supporting my report objective—are clear to my reader. Examine my new outline. Based on my thesis, I have one negative element and three positive ones. This tells me I may need to offset cost with benefits in a contrast method. I can't bury the $4,000,000, but I can soften its initial impact. Bad news must still come first, but I can introduce it in manageable increments.

  I. Additional hardware
     A. Cost/Speed
     B. Cost/Operations
     C. Cost/Customer

Now, I'm saying: "Yes, increased capability is expensive, *but,* look what we get for the money.—Yes, Operations will have to bite the bullet for x amount, *but* look what they're getting.—Yes, the Customer will have to pay more, *but* she is going to love end result." There are still no guarantees the reader will accept my recommendation, but at least, he will see the total picture before making a decision.

Briefing can also ensure persuasive arrangement if my thesis is con or negative: "The XYZ Corporation should not purchase additional hardware next year." I probably would begin with the same outline I had when my thesis was positive, and I would brief in the same way.

I. Additional hardware

  A. Customer

  B. Operations

  C. Speed

  D. Cost

I. Additional hardware will

  A. facilitate new and larger
     system required by customer.

  B. increase efficiency and
     reduce cost in operations.

  Additional hardware is

  C. faster and more efficient.

  D. too costly for the approved
     budget.

Again, I find I must rearrange subheadings A, B, and C, just to avoid confusing repetition of material. Now, however, *Cost,* which was the bad news in my first example and had to appear first, should remain last. In this way, I recognize the advantages of additional hardware, but my final point supports my negative premise.

  I. Additional hardware
     A. Speed
     B. Operations
     C. Customer
     D. Cost

Here, based on my objective, I have only one positive element, and three negative ones. Using briefing, I can see my reader may be so influenced by benefits that costing will not have the impact I desire. In this instance, I could decide to *shadowbox*—surround the three elements that work against my thesis with the one element that corroborates it.

    I. Additional hardware at cost of (amount)
        A. Speed
        B. Operations
        C. Customer
        D. Cost

My reader now views all the advantages in light of the primary disadvantage, and my final point reinforces my negative stance.

I can, of course, again use the contrast method. Remembering "bad news first," I simply reverse its order.

    I. Additional hardware
        A. Speed/Cost
        B. Operations/Cost
        C. Customer/Cost

My erasure here says: "Yes, we can get this capability, *but* look at what it costs.—Yes, Operations will benefit, *but* not enough to justify the initial expense.—Yes, the Customer wants this system, *but* she can't afford it."

Learn to brief any outline based on your original definition of the purpose of your report. With practice, the technique becomes almost second-nature. You'll find you feel more comfortable with the writing process itself, and the resulting report organization will be better. Also, it takes far less time to evaluate each element of your report *prior to writing* than to rearrange and rewrite a finished document.

22

The Waste Basket Method—A Unique Shortcut to Effective Reporting

The techniques of report organization that we've discussed so far *do* work. They are, however, somewhat time-consuming, even with practice.

Fortunately, once you understand the principles behind organizing report structure—including briefing—it is possible to simplify and shorten the entire process. The Waste Basket Method is my personal approach and it's a great way to "cheat" and still come up with a highly successful document.

Go back for a moment to exhibit D outlining, "The Systematic Approach to Report Preparation," page 163.

Now that you've reviewed the necessary steps, you're ready for the Waste Basket exercise. All you will need when you actually begin to write a report is a piece or pieces of scrap paper, pen or pencil.

Remember, your first task as a competent report writer is to spell out your report objective. Once you've defined it mentally to your satisfaction, write it down at the top of the page.

Your next step is a valid analysis of available data. As you proceed with the analytical process, list your facts on the same sheet of paper, directly under your statement of purpose. This not only aids your analysis, but ensures that no data are lost or forgotten until too late for them to be of value.

Also, as you analyze the data, you are coming up with alternative courses of action. List these recommendations and conclusions in a third section immediately following your data list.

Once you complete this procedure—depending on the size and complexity of your report—your scrap paper should look something like this:

SAMPLE REPORT

PURPOSE
To demonstrate the need for new personnel—2 Systems Analysts
                                             5 Programmer/Analysts

DATA

8 approved new projects in the department.

300 additional person days required.

ETAs are *not* flexible, yet not feasible with current staff.

Accelerated training program is now available.

Work space available at present location.

Current personnel budget too small.

RECOMMENDATIONS

Immediate recruitment of experienced personnel.

Scheduling of training program.

Assignment of department personnel to work with personnel department in interviewing.

Increase in personnel budget.

System for directing new personnel to projects.

Let's assume I'm actually going to write the report shown in our sample. Here is how I would proceed, using the Waste Basket Method.

My second most important decision in writing any Management Report is still selection of the report format best-suited to my thesis, either PSYCHOLOGICAL or LOGICAL. (See Chapter 20, "Report Formats" page 178.)

Review the purpose of the sample report. Based on what I hope to accomplish, I would select the PSYCHOLOGICAL format. Think about it. My objective in the sample is actually a conclusion. The current work situation as I see it is what's prompting the report in the first place. My analysis is more crucial to the end result than the facts supporting my decision.

I know the most important element in the PSYCHOLOGICAL format is the Conclusions and Recommendations section. I would, therefore, move directly to the recommendations list on my piece of scrap paper and rate each recommendation in order of *my* priority. I find it easiest to use numbers, jotted in the left-hand margin.

RECOMMENDATIONS

1. Immediate recruitment of experienced personnel.
5. Scheduling of training program.
3. Assignment of department personnel to work with personnel department in interviewing.
2. Increase in personnel budget.
4. System for directing new personnel to projects.

Once I have established priority, I never proceed with more than *two* recommendations at a time. Trying to work with everything I hope to say in my entire report can be overwhelming and slow things considerably. So, I pull out my two most important recommendations:

1. Immediate recruitment of experienced personnel.
2. Increase in personnel budget.

Now, each writer must go by his or her own judgment. In looking at the sample, you may not have rated these two recommendations in the order I did. That doesn't matter—as long as you did pinpoint these two recommendations as highest in priority. Here are my reasons for selecting these two and sequencing them as I did. I looked at my report purpose and asked myself two questions:

One, what do I need?

I need people.

Two, what do I need to get what I need?

I need money.

I can't go by our "bad news first" rule here, as both these recommendations will probably be considered bad news by my reader.

As you remember from Chapter 19, "Techniques of Professional Report Writers," I also cannot make any recommendation that cannot be supported by data. My next step then must be to identify data that will justify each of my two most important recommendations. To do so, I move to the data list on my scrap paper. This time I use numbers corresponding to the respective recommendations in the margin and note those facts that corroborate each.

    DATA
1. 8 approved new projects in the department.
1. 300 additional person days required.
2. 1. ETAs are *not* flexible, yet not feasible with current staff.
    Accelerated training program is now available.
    Work space available at present location.
  2. Current personnel budget too small.

My Waste Basket outline now looks like this:

1. Immediate recruitment of experienced personnel.

  A. 8 approved new projects in the department.
  B. 300 person days required.
  C. ETAs *not* flexible, yet not feasible with current staff.

2. Increase in personnel budget.

   A. Current personnel budget too small.
   B. ETAs *not* flexible, yet not feasible with current staff.

Let's examine my choices. Certainly, under recommendation # 1, I had to provide my reader with the "stage-setting" information of 8 approved new projects, requiring 300 person days. Develop a critical eye for data, however. Three hundred person days only justifies how many new employees in the course of one year? One? One and a half? Two, if you're lucky? How many am I asking for? One look at the report objective tells you I'm requesting *seven*. I must anticipate my reader's mental question, "Why seven people for only 300 person days of work?" The answer, of course, is that I'm in a time bind. My ETAs are not flexible, and the 300 days can't be spread out as a year's work for one or two employees.

Under recommendation # 2, the first fact listed is inevitable. Not only is it "bad news first," but if the current personnel budget were not too small, I wouldn't need to recommend *any* increase. I do have to go one step further, however. Most DP department's budgets could absorb one or two additional people. Again, I'm asking for *seven,* and I need them immediately. To justify my second most important recommendation and convey its urgency, I must re-emphasize one crucial fact—the inflexibility of the project ETAs.

OK. I now have noted my two most vital recommendations, and I have data to support them. I understand and have organized *my* viewpoint. What, however, about my reader's? We know that anticipating reader objections and probable reaction is essential to effective written communication. I still need to evaluate my Waste Basket outline from my reader's frame of reference.

I start by asking myself, "Is there any alternative open to my reader other than to accept my two most important recommendations?" Look at the supporting data carefully, and I believe you'll see there is. My reader could come back to me and say, "Seven people is impossible—*change the ETAs.*" If you check the sample, you'll see I have just identified a possibility I had overlooked in my original thinking. Now, I must determine how viable an alternative it is. Look at data A under recommendation #1. Those eight new projects are *approved.* They must have been approved with the ETAs already established. Furthermore, they were probably approved by whom? That's right, the person I'm addressing in my report. I now know I must mention this alternative in order to assure my reader I considered it. I also know, however, I can't count on this as a solution. If the ETAs are to change, it's my reader's job to change them—not mine. Past experience tells me he or she is not likely to do so.

Next, I ask myself, "Would my reader have any questions I have not answered?" Again, critically examine the outline. I have told my reader I need seven people to do 300 person days of work because of inflexible ETAs. I realize the ETAs are not likely to change. Wouldn't the reader of my report then want to know what happens to those seven people once the 300 person days are expended? He or she is not going to look kindly on their sitting around doing nothing and still costing money.

Anticipating such reader reaction tells me one of two things. I must *add* a recommendation proposing some future utilization of the seven people after the eight projects are completed. Or, if I can't come up with adequate future placement for the new employees, I must *change* my first recommendation. Something else—perhaps the enlisting of temporary help—would certainly be more valid.

If I can justify seven new employees beyond the eight projects, my Waste Basket outline is now expanded.

1. Immediate recruitment of new personnel.
   A. 8 approved new projects in the department.
   B. 300 additional person days required.
   C. ETAs *not* flexible, yet not feasible with current staff.

2. Increase in personnel budget.
   A. Current personnel budget too small.
   B. ETAs *not* flexible, yet not feasible with current staff.

3. Utilization of new employees after completion of 8 projects.

Possible alternative: Change the ETAs.

If I am unable to place the new employees beyond the current workload, my Waste Basket outline must change.

1. Hire consulting or temporary personnel.
   A. 8 approved new projects in the department.
   B. 300 additional person days required.
   C. ETAs *not* flexible, yet not feasible with current staff.

2. Increase in personnel budget.
   A. Current personnel budget too small.
   B. ETAs *not* flexible, yet not feasible with current staff.

Possible alternative: Change the ETAs.

In either case, I have now assured effective organization and the validity of the most important aspects of my report. By using the Waste Basket approach, I discovered a possibility I had not previously considered and evaluated its potential. I also found I either needed to add a missing recommendation or completely revamp my first and most important one. Certainly, the time to make organizational decisions like these is before I distribute an incomplete or invalid report.

Now, I am ready to proceed with my next two most important recommendations and repeat exactly the same Waste Basket appraisal. Before I include the recommendations I originally rated as #3 and #4 in my outline, however, I am going to ask myself this crucial question: In order to write a good result-oriented report, *do I need to go any further than what I have developed so far?*

I don't.

Examine my remaining recommendations once again and see if you can determine why I can and should stop right here. Important as they may be, each of the unused recommendations is dependent on my reader's saying yes to what I have proposed so far. Once I have an affirmative response, they may form the basis for a report on actual steps to be taken. At this point, however, they are extraneous. Why take my valuable time to write them or my reader's limited time to review them until the primary decision is reached?

Consider what I have done. Most report writers estimate one hour to an hour and a half per recommendation in figuring their time for total preparation of a report. By applying the Waste Basket Method, I've gone from five recommendations to two or three—one of which I hadn't even thought of in my original planning. I've also gone from six identified facts to four crucial ones, and I've determined a previously unconsidered reader alternative. The Waste Basket Method only took perhaps ten minutes of my time. Yet, I cut a potential six-hour assignment down to about three hours. Also, my end product is better.

Now, this is a simple example. With many reports, I will have more than two (or three) recommendations. I would then take the next two and work through them. I may even have to add two more. Certainly, my initial investment of time in the Waste Basket Method will be greater with more complex reports. As you remember from "Techniques of Professional Report Writers," however, my goal would be five major points—ten at the outside. Even when the Waste Basket Method takes longer, I can cut my overall effort at least in half. Imagine the savings of time and improved quality when writing large-scale reports such as a Feasibility Study or Proposal.

The Waste Basket Method also works equally well with the LOGICAL format. The steps are simply reversed. The most important element in the LOGICAL is the data. Therefore, I would start with my data section, rating each fact in order of my priority. As I did with the recommendations in the PSYCHOLOGICAL, I would then pull out my two most important pieces of data. The data must lead to a recommendation or conclusion, so I then move to my recommendation list. Using the numbers as I did in the sample, I would assign pertinent recommendations to the critical data in my outline. The same questions are asked to ascertain reader frame of reference. The same evaluation criteria are used to determine when all necessary material has been included.

In fact, the Waste Basket Method does not need to be limited to report writing, either PSYCHOLOGICAL or LOGICAL. I use it for memorandums, business letters—whenever I'm stuck in preparing a document or unsure of the sense and effectiveness of any written material.

One final advantage to the Waste Basket Method. It is ideally suited to the team concept. Try it when a report, such as a Feasibility Study or Proposal, must represent group effort. The team meets, each starting with a piece of scrap paper, and the technique is followed, accompanied by discussion. When the process is completed, all members of the team have agreed on defined objective, priorities, recommended actions, and the impact of the supporting facts. This not only makes for excellent reports, it ensures cooperation and solid understanding between individual members once the team swings into action.

Index